Migrants and Minorities

Socialist History 23

Rivers Oram Press
London, Sydney and Chicago

Editorial Board

Stefan Berger	Elizabeth Fidlon	Willie Thompson
John Callaghan	David Howell	Mike Waite
Andy Croft	Neville Kirk	
Allison Drew	David Parker	

Editorial Advisers: Noreen Branson, Eric Hobsbawm, Monty Johnstone, Victor Kiernan, David Marquand, Ben Pimlott, Pat Thane

Editorial Enquiries: Kevin Morgan, Department of Government, University of Manchester M13 9PL or kevin.morgan@man.ac.uk.

Reviews Enquiries: John Callaghan, School of Humanities, Languages and Social Sciences, University of Wolverhampton, Wulfruna Street, Wolverhampton WV1 1PB or j.callaghan@wlv.ac.uk

Socialist History 23 was edited by Stephen Woodhams, Julie Johnson, Matthew Worley, Kevin Morgan, Lesley Harding

Published in 2003
by Rivers Oram Press, an imprint of Rivers Oram Publishers Ltd
144 Hemingford Road, London N1 1DE

Distributed in the USA by
Independent Publishers Group, Franklin Street, Chicago IL 60610
Distributed in Australia and New Zealand by
UNIReps, University of New South Wales, Sydney, NSW 2052

Set in Garamond by NJ Design
and printed in Great Britain by T.J. International Ltd, Padstow

This edition copyright © 2003 Socialist History Society
The articles are copyright © 2003 Keith Copley, Shivdeep Singh Grewal, Stephen Hipkin, Cronain O'Kelly

No part of this journal may be produced in any form, except for the quotation of brief passages in criticism, without the written permission of the publishers The right of the contributors to be identified as the authors has been asserted by them in accordance with the Copyright, Designs and Patents Act 1988

British Library Cataloguing in Publication Data
A catalogue record for this publication is available from the British Library
ISBN 1 85489 154 5 (hb)
ISBN 1 85489 155 3 (pb)
ISSN 0969 4331

Contents

Notes on Contributors	v
Editorial	vii
Capital of the 1970s? Southall and the conjuncture of 23 April 1979 Shivdeep Singh Grewal	1
Ireland and British Politics Keith Copley	35
Labour's Irish Questions 1918–81 Cronain O'Kelly	54
Property, Economic Interest and the Configuration of Rural Conflict in Sixteenth and Seventeenth-Century England Stephen Hipkin	67
Rodney Hilton 1916–2002 David Parker	89
Reviews	91

Books to be remembered (6)
Alan Winnington, *Breakfast with Mao. Memoirs of a foreign correspondent* (John Saville)

Ralph Darlington and Dave Lyddon, *Glorious Summer. Class struggle in Britain, 1972* (Mike Jones)

Andrew Thorpe, *The British Communist Party and Moscow 1920–43* (Kevin Morgan)

Duncan Tanner, Pat Thane and Nick Tiratsoo (eds), *Labour's First Century* (Noreen Branson)

Kathleen Burk, *Troublemaker. The life and history of A.J.P. Taylor* (Willie Thompson)

Ross M. Martin, *The Lancashire Giant. David Shackleton Labour leader and civil servant* (Peter Kentfield)

Noel Thompson, *Left in the Wilderness. The political economy of British democratic socialism since 1979* (John Callaghan)

Notes on Contributors

Shivdeep Singh Grewal is a researcher on EU social policy at the University of Essex. In 1998 he co-produced, with Ross Dalziel, a video documentary *Remembering Southall April 23rd 1979*.

Keith Copley is a researcher and writer in social history.

Stephen Hipkin teaches in the Department of History at Canterbury Christchurch University College. He has published several articles on property relations in rural Kent in the sixteenth, seventeenth and eighteenth centuries and recently co-edited *Romney Marsh. Coastal and landscape change through the ages* (Oxford, 2002).

Cronain O'Kelly teaches politics and history at the Open University.

Editorial

Contrary to popular myth and media image, migrants and minorities are nothing new to the British Isles. In reality, the whole population of the islands is composed of just such people, and in recent years the recognition of complexity has provided a major feature in the work of diverse writers from Linda Colley to Salman Rushdie and Raphael Samuel. In this issue, *Socialist History* provides a range of different perspectives on some of the peoples who have inhabited various parts of the islands, and yet each is more than a story of migration and settlement. Instead, in their different ways our first three articles all address the political and economic relations between dominant institutions and subordinate peoples, examining the means of that domination and the racist constructions of selected peoples.

The first article exactly meets these varied features, examining one historical moment before moving outwards to the longer history of different political groups, the state and the extreme right. Shivdeep Grewal's article on Southall derives from a documentary film, *Remembering Southall April 23rd 1979* (1998) which he co-produced. His paper starts from the single conjuncture of this date which saw the intersection of prominent political conflicts of the time and the lives of local residents. In developing his thesis, Grewal draws upon the Western Marxism of Walter Benjamin. He cites Benjamin's approach which seizes on the peripheral fragments and 'finding in them the distillation of the zeitgeist particularly from the perspective of oppressed people'. The article consists of five logical sections. The first recovers the events of 23 April 1979 (St George's Day) when Southall was invaded by members of the National Front, which had been granted permission to hold an election meeting by the Conservative-led Ealing Borough Council. Evidently, at the end of the 1970s playing the 'race' card could still work in inner West London, as it still does at the western fringes of the metropolitan area.[1]

Grewal continues the article with four sections each focusing on one of the major actors who participated in the events of the day. Beginning with Southall's own political groups and their place in the wider community, he then reviews the very broad church of the left in Britain and suggests that the traditional implicit racism of sections of the left, particularly the trade unions, was in the 1970s being challenged by the 'New Left'. Grewal's fourth section reviews the rise of the authoritarian right, a phenomenon inextricably associated with the rise of Margaret Thatcher, and yet inconceivable without a deep cultural shift to an authoritarian 'world view' on the part of a large section of the population. Central to this was 'race', with any person not perceived as 'English' being automatically defined as an enemy. Grewal's final section shows how this rise of the authoritarian right was reflected by the decline of the extreme racist right, as the National Front was overtaken by Thatcherism.

Two of our articles focus on Ireland. Keith Copley's contribution focuses on relations between Ireland and Britain during the period of Chartism. Situating the relationship in its imperial context of the time, Copley first explores the economic consequences of the colonial relationship, which he argues meant the shaping of Ireland's economy to serve Britain's interests. He then examines the English image of the Irish and Celtic populations and argues that during the infamous potato famine this even ran to the extent of blaming a supposed Irish character for the poverty of the peasantry. If this deliberate denigration of the Irish needs to be set in the context of hardening racist and imperialist attitudes, Copley's discussion of the relations between Irish and English workers suggests that there was not only friction but the involvement of Irish workers in radical activity and especially Chartism. Citing the protests of radicals in England at government coercion in Ireland, he ends on a less pessimistic note.

Cronain O'Kelly's contribution examines the relations of the labour movement in Britain with Irish republicanism. Covering the period from the end of the First World War to the Good Friday Agreement, O'Kelly offers a systematic critique of the Labour Party leadership focusing on the issues of partition; the character of the state in the six counties; and the revival of republican action since 1970. He also recalls some less remembered events in the history of Irish republicanism, including its military campaign from 1956 to 1962. Arguing the republican case for the illegitimacy of any government, whether of 'south' or 'north', following the British imposition of partition in 1921, O'Kelly is drawn to a pessimistic conclusion in the wake of the Good Friday Agreement: 'there are still republicans but no republicanism.'

In our final article, Stephen Hipkin looks at property relations and rural conflict in early modern England. Taking as his reference point Robert Brenner's 1976 essay on class structure and economic development in pre-industrial Europe, Hipkin suggests that the situation in this period was more complex than Brenner's positing of class structure and class conflict as the 'key to the problem of long-term economic development' would suggest. Hipkin seeks to demonstrate this showing how economic and legal circumstances made for a problematic class structure with relations variant on such matters as copyholds and freeholds, and ownership of land and ownership of use-rights. In beginning with the proposition that class is to be defined by 'objective relations of production' and not consciousness of that relationship, he engages with a debate with which readers of this journal will already be familiar, dating back to Edward Thompson's magisterial 'Preface' to his *Making of the English Working Class* and beyond.

We are particularly pleased to extend the journal's normal chronological range with the articles by Keith Copley, and especially that of Stephen Hipkin. Other contributions on periods falling outside our customary focus on the late nineteenth and twentieth centuries will be gratefully received. Readers will also notice that the journal now has an editorial board, which first met in October of last year and which we hope will help involve more people in the running of the journal as well as guide its overall direction. Further names are being added to the board, and in the meantime we are particularly pleased to welcome the involvement of John Callaghan, who will be taking the main responsibility for reviews. Thanks are therefore due to Stephen Woodhams, for his efforts with reviews over the past three years, as well as for guest-editing the current issue. Thanks too to our editorial advisers, whose assistance with and feedback on the journal continues to be appreciated.

Note

1. In the 2001 General Election a candidate for the BNP stood in the Borough of Hillingdon and received 547 votes.

Socialist History Titles

Requests for back issues to ro@riversoram.demon.co.uk

Previous issues of Socialist History include:

13 Imperialism and Internationalism
...Victor Kiernan on empires; Anna Davin on immigration; Ralph Russell on Indian nationalism...
1 85489 107 3

14 The Future of History
...roundtable discussion with Jim Sharpe, Peter Jones, Mike Savage, Eileen Yeo, Kevin Morgan and Richard Evans...
1 85489 109 X

15 Visions of the Future
...David Purdy on utopian thought; Philip Coupland on utopia in British political culture; Maureen Speller on the future in science fiction...
1 85489 115 4

16 America and the Left
...David Howell on syndicalism; Neville Kirk on American exceptionalism; Kevin Morgan on the British left and America...
1 85489 117 0

17 International Labour History
...Sheila Rowbotham on working class women's narratives; Karen Hunt on internationalism and socialist women; Paul Kelemen on Labour's Africa...
1 85489 119 7

18 Cultures and Politics
...Matthew Worley on the Third Period; Andrew Whitehead on Red London; Martin Wasserman on Kafka as industrial reformer...
1 85489 123 5

19 Life Histories
...Richard Pankhurst on Sylvia Pankhurst and anti-fascism; Andy Croft on Randall Swingler; Malcolm Chase interviews John Saville on the *DLB*...
1 85489 129 4

20 Contested Legacies
...Mark Bevir on socialism and the state; Matt Perry on the Hunger Marches; David Renton and Martin Durham debate women, gender and fascism...
1 85489 135 9

21 Red Lives
...Till Kössler on West German communists; Margreet Schrevel on a Dutch communist children's club; Tauno Saarela on characters in Finnish communist magazines...
1 85489 141 3

22 Revolutions and Revolutionaries
...John Newsinger on Irish Labour; Allison Drew on experiences of the gulag; Edward Acton, Monty Johnstone, Boris Kagarlitsky, Francis King and Hillel Ticktin on the significance of 1917...
1 85489 141 3

Capital of the 1970s?
Southall and the conjuncture of 23 April 1979

Shivdeep Singh Grewal

Accounts of the police violence, fascist provocation and community resistance that shook Southall, a town in West London and, since the 1950s, one of the most prominent Asian communities in the UK, on 23 April 1979 fall into broadly two camps. By far the most numerous are those found in histories of postwar Britain where the disturbances, or 'riots' (depending on the political complexion of the author), are presented as a footnote to the ongoing narrative of race relations. In the second, far smaller, category are accounts from the streets themselves: amalgams of reportage, oral history and archival research such as the report from the National Council for Civil Liberties (NCCL), the impassioned *Southall: The Birth of a Black Community*, or the feminist perspectives of Southall Black Sisters (SBS).

Between the two poles, those of history exclusively from 'above' or 'below', reside the urban myths and collective memories of 23 April 1979: a conjuncture of innumerable influences, from the prosaic to the world-historical, which were juxtaposed and fused together at the time to endure to the present day as a parallel historical record restricted to anecdote and memory rather than the permanence of print. Hence, in the course of discussion with local residents[1] present on the day, it is not uncommon for recollections to elide spatial and temporal details with those of disparate other phenomena of concern to the community at the time and since: memories of the community resistance of 23 April 1979 often merge with those of other anti-racist struggles in the town,[2] the events were a central influence on the personal and political identity of second generation Asians in Southall and elsewhere, and the day itself offers a snapshot of national and international political tendencies of the time of which right-wing extremism and incipient Thatcherism are only the most obvious examples.

It is the nature of this conjuncture that I will explore in the course of this paper based on the intuition that the events and experiences in this small West London town were uniquely illustrative of among the most pressing political questions of the day. In particular, I will argue that the solidarity and militancy that arose in the Southall of the 1970s in response to the collective experience of racial violence facilitated the growth of a uniquely progressive political culture, a cosmopolitan modernity that would sadly be undermined in the 1980s.

Insofar as such a perspective can be adopted as a scholarly method, the idiosyncratic 'historical materialism' of Walter Benjamin offers an encouraging antecedent. Employed implicitly throughout his work, and stated in detail in his *Theses on the Philosophy of History*,[3] Benjamin's approach consisted of focussing on peripheral fragments, whether in the form of cultural ephemera or obscure events, of the dominant version of history and, finding in them a distillation of the zeitgeist, particularly from the perspective of oppressed peoples. The relevant fragments were deemed to offer a glimpse of a richer, more hopeful modernity. Hence the approach demands hermeneutic sensitivity, the selection for study of objects or occurrences that fulfil these exacting requirements.[4]

> Materialist historiography…is based on a constructive principle. Thinking involves not only the flow of thoughts but also their arrest as well. Where thinking suddenly stops in a configuration pregnant with tensions, it gives birth to a monad. A historical materialist approaches a historical subject only where he encounters it as a monad. In this structure he recognises the sign of a Messianic cessation of happening, or, put differently, a revolutionary chance in the fight for the oppressed past.[5]

Inspired by Benjamin's practice of this method in a seminal 1935 essay proclaiming the Paris of Baudelaire and the inchoate processes of modernity to be the 'Capital of the Nineteenth-Century', I have chosen to focus on the spatio-temporal environs of Southall, particularly during the conjuncture of 23 April 1979, as similarly, if on a more modest scale, representing a 'Capital of the 1970s'. I will argue that the conjuncture saw the intersection between prominent political conflicts of the day and the lives of the local residents in a singularly significant historical-phenomenological moment, a 'monad' heraldic of far more than would at first appear. In particular, this monad saw the culmination and conjuncture of tensions between four historical actors that had been in conflict throughout the postwar period, especially in the 1970s: Britain's black communities, particularly the second generation of Southall's Asian youth who were born in the UK; the radical, mostly extra-parliamentary, left and the trade unions whose attitudes toward ethnic minorities and the processes of decolonisation had undergone a complex evolution with the growth of the 'New Left' in the 1960s; the elite forces of state, government, police, judiciary, and mass media whose gradual adoption of 'New Right' prescriptions was facilitated by the crises of the 1970s; and finally the, predominantly extra-parliamentary, groupings of the extreme right, from the Racial Preservation Societies (RPS) to the National Front (NF).

In the introduction to this article I will present a breakdown of the events of 23 April 1979. I will continue through the next four sections by following the historical evolution of each of the four actors who participated in the events of the day up to the conjuncture and by reflecting briefly on their fates in the changed climate of the 1980s. In each of the four cases, I will argue that the events of the conjuncture either contributed to, or coincided with, a change in the fortunes of the actor in question, such as in the cases of the 'remarshalling' of elite power or of accelerated fascist decline after 1979.

Introduction

A small town in the south west corner of the London Borough of Ealing, Southall was able by 1976 to boast a population of whom 46 per cent could claim descent from the New Commonwealth and Pakistan against a national average of 3.5 per cent.[6]

With a valiant history of resistance to racial discrimination and attack, both from the first generation of settlers and their increasingly militant offspring, it is unsurprising that a decision by the local Tory-led council to allow the neo-fascist NF to hold an election meeting in the local town hall on the 23 April 1979, the incendiary date of Saint George's day, caused anger and dismay to Southall's residents. With no support or prospect of electoral success in the town since the early 1970s, the meeting was clearly intended to promote racial tension.

Yet the insensitivity of the local council was soon matched by a vigorous, though ultimately unsuccessful, campaign by local community groups to stop the meeting. Among the measures called for by local residents and activists, including those of the Indian Workers Association (IWA), were the decision to hold a protest march for 'unity and peace' on 22 April and a half-day strike and sit-down protest outside the town hall from 5 p.m. the following day. Calls for a protest march on 23 April made by groups such as the Socialist Workers Party (SWP), Anti-Nazi League (ANL) and Socialist Unity, a group headed by Tariq Ali[7] which planned to campaign for election in Southall in the coming election, were turned down by local groupings in favour of the sit-down protest. Telegrams were also sent to the prime minister, the home secretary, and the chairman of the Commission for Racial Equality emphasising the danger of violent confrontation if the meeting were allowed to go ahead.[8]

The Southall Youth Movement (SYM), one of the few groups that declined to participate in the IWA coordinated protests, decided to form its own independent picket near the town hall before the start of the meeting. All of the activities proposed by the various groups were reported to the police although the latter neglected in turn to convey their exact attitudes and intentions back to community leaders.[9]

The unity and peace demonstration of 22 April proved a success, marshalling 5000 people in a dignified march to Ealing Borough town hall. Yet, despite their apparent acquiescence to the requests of the local residents, the police proved to have a quite different attitude on the day of the NF meeting when they prevented any kind of protest from going ahead.

A portent of the conflict to come was already apparent in the council's crass decision to fly the Union Jack, a symbol that the NF had claimed for itself as a party badge and one, moreover, that was not suitable for that one day in the year,[10] over the town hall. Hours before the planned demonstrations, two and three-quarter thousand members of the Metropolitan Police force arrived in Southall and proceeded to occupy the whole of the town centre (including the town hall area). A significant proportion of this occupying force were members of the Special Patrol Group (SPG), a quasi-military grouping conceived in the context of the industrial and terrorist violence of the preceding decade and hence wholly unsuited to the policing of a small, peaceful civilian protest. Claiming the need to create a 'sterile area' at the centre of the town, rhetoric characteristic of the government's counter-insurgency policies toward public protest since the 1960s, the police prevented the protesters from demonstrating outside of the town hall and ensured the passage of sixty NF members attending the meeting. Though a nominally 'public' election meeting, NF stewards unlawfully prevented individual members of the local community from attending and even barred a *Daily Mirror* reporter, Kevin O'Lone, from entering on the charge that his paper 'supports these niggers and is a Labour rag'.[11]

As the evening wore on an increasing number of arrests were made, among them many of the demonstration stewards who had diligently been maintaining order and calm earlier in the day. By now the police had penned the remaining demonstrators between double cordons on each of the four roads leading into the sterile area of the town centre. Arrests continued to be made and accounts from the hundreds of eyewitnesses who gave evidence for the NCCL report suggested that, in the words of clergyman Reverend Theo Samuels, police 'discipline had broken down' by the early evening.[12] At one point an unmarked coach manned by a civilian driver and a police officer drove towards a particularly large crowd of penned-in demonstrators from behind at approximately 30 miles per hour. Witnesses note that it was miraculous that no one was killed,[13] yet further charges by police vans followed.[14]

A detailed account of the sheer scale of the brutality and indiscipline shown by the police toward demonstrators and bystanders alike is given in the report by the NCCL. Two further events must, however, be taken into account if the full magnitude of the violation of the local community, by police and fascists alike, is to be appreciated.

At about 7.45 pm Blair Peach, a teacher from East London and member of the ANL, was struck on the head by an assailant widely believed to have been a member of the SPG.[15] He died from his injuries at 12.10 am in the course of emergency surgery.[16] While the coroner's report noted that the head injuries he received were not compatible with the sort of truncheons officially employed by the police on the day, rather being suggestive of a lead weighted rubber cosh or similar weapon, searches on 5 June of the lockers of SPG officers who had been on duty in Southall revealed an arsenal of correspondingly non-standard weapons including crowbars, knives, a whip, a leather encased truncheon, a metal truncheon, a pickaxe handle and a brass handle.[17] To this day, no police officer active on 23 April has been charged with Blair Peach's murder.

Some of the worst police violence was targeted at the premises of a local community group, Peoples Unite, the culmination of a lengthy campaign of intimidation towards its members.[18] The Peoples Unite premises had been agreed upon as a medical centre and, apparently without the consent of the members, as an unofficial meeting and coordination centre for groups such as the ANL and Socialist Unity. As the day wore on, the house began to fill with local residents and activists unable, due to the police barricades, to get home, until the house held in the region of 100 people. Having broken into the house, police wielding truncheons and riot shields proceeded to mount a frenzied attack on the people inside, concentrating significant attention on those in the medical centre and subjecting all occupants to a barrage of blows as they descended the stairs and were ejected from the building. Clarence Baker, a prominent member of Peoples Unite, received a blood clot on the brain from a blow he received and was kept under hourly hospital observation for a week afterwards. Baker noted that the basement storage rooms of the house, locked during the demonstration, were also broken into by the police and that the musical equipment therein, valued at approximately £10,000, had been completely destroyed. The attack on the persons and property of Peoples Unite were to prove so traumatic that activities at the house could not continue afterwards. Adding insult to injury, the Tory-led council refused to consider compensation for the destruction of equipment.[19] Of the thirty-seven occupants of the building interviewed about the day's events, thirty-one, including Tariq Ali, testified to incomprehensible levels of violence and indiscipline from the police.[20]

The dismay and outrage experienced by the community continued to be felt for many years after the events, not least because of the trials that followed where 345 people,[21] the largest number in a single day since the mass CND sit-downs of the early 1960s, were charged. The number was so great that most local residents could claim to have had some connection with one or more of the defendants. The proceedings were also considered to be unfair due to the practice of trying many of the defendants collectively in a 'riot court' and, through the hostile conduct of the stipendiary magistrates chosen to try them who were known in advance to have harsh views on conviction and sentence. Ultimately, the effect of the violence on the day, and the harsh treatment of the accused in the trials that followed, would be to weaken the Asian community's faith in the police and the judicial system which had previously been seen as above reproach.[22]

Yet the events of 23 April would also serve to strengthen the already formidable levels of solidarity within Asian communities such as Southall. This was immediately apparent on 28 April when approximately 15,000 people took part in a silent, dignified march in memory of Blair Peach, and in solidarity demonstrations organised across the country in the following days. The account of 28 April given by community relations officer Martyn Grubb provides a sense of the occasion:

> Above all…because of its orderliness. Secondly, because of its size…People—ordinary housewives and children, ordinary Southall families —were coming out of their front doors as the march passed and joining. They were not just all Indians though the majority were. There were people of every race and colour. It was quiet. Just before it got to the place where Blair Peach died a loudspeaker asked everyone to maintain silence. I left the march for a time at that spot and watched the march go by. That was where I realised it was so big…I felt it was a very healing thing—not just neutral but positively good .[23]

In particular, the youth of Southall had begun to display a level of political will and organisation that would see them taking on the task of defending the community in a more assertive style than that of their parents. This determination led to the successful defence of the town, and the final defeat of the marauding skinheads who had periodically menaced residents since the late 1960s, in the 'second round' of clashes in 1981. This time, a fascist rock concert held at the Hambrough Tavern provoked a massive response from the SYM and its allies who burned down the pub, thereby ridding the town of its last racist enclave. The radical spirit unleashed on 23 April would also have the effect of galvanising activism in the area, leading to the formation of the Southall Monitoring Group (SMG) in 1979 and SBS in November of the same year.

A public sphere and its New Social Movements

In the *Structural Transformation of the Public Sphere*,[24] Jürgen Habermas charts the evolution of the bourgeois public sphere, a set of interlinked fora for the open discussion of state policy among 'informed outsiders', from its origins in the coffee houses and salons of eighteenth-century Europe, to its decline in the twentieth century with the encroachment of organised interests concerned to modulate public opinion. The longevity of this public sphere was assisted to a significant extent by the existence of organs of communication, such as newspapers and letters, to ensure the circulation of ideas. The importance of such media is further illustrated by James Curran and Jean Seaton in their analysis of the rise and decline of the radical working class press in nineteenth-century England, a medium finally eclipsed when, having endured legal measures designed to curtail its influence, it was undermined by the sheer costs of competition and production in an era of the increasing 'industrialisation of the press'.[25] As with the coffee houses of the eighteenth century, the working-class press contributed to the growth of class consciousness and unity, a shared value system, and a sense of the potential power of the inchoate classes, bourgeoisie and proletariat respectively, to conceive and bring about social change.[26]

In the truncated timescale of the decades between their postwar arrival and the radicalism of their second generation offspring, a similarly fertile community identity and political consciousness arose in Southall through the growth of a distinct public sphere, complete with the fora for interaction and the organs of communication on which it was based, and with the growth of correspondingly innovative forms of political mobilisation.

The latter of these tendencies is conceived of by Gilroy as the movement from primarily socialistic forms of organisation, with the emancipation of each worker's labour as their primary motivation, to the rise of New Social Movements (NSM) more concerned with the symbolic reproduction and autonomy of an ethnic community.[27] Hence, an NSM can be regarded as the reified expression of the political will that arises in a correspondingly cosmopolitan, modern public sphere. As I will argue in the course of this section, the growth of Southall's NSMs was an open ended, and even reversible, process initiated by the IWAs and continued with the youth protest of the late 1970s.

Indeed, the very heterogeneity of influences that came together in Southall, from secular, democratic and socialist traditions to various forms of collective worship, have meant that the community has undergone almost continuous evolution and change, not least in the extent to which it has absorbed English cultural and political influences. This rapid development of community fora and political organisations was given a renewed stimulus with the coming of age of Southall's youth. Hence, the period up to the conjuncture of 1979 was marked by the increasingly direct political action of the second generation in relation to both police and fascist harassment, and, the development of modern forms of political expression and mobilisation concentrated on the notion of black unity and struggle. The latter innovations paralleled those of the New Left in the 1960s and 1970s with its youthful demographic composition and linkage of decolonisation struggles to those of radicals in western urban centres.

Yet, as I will also argue in this section, the very 'porosity' of a public sphere such as that of Southall contributes a vulnerability to corrosive influences alongside an openness to sources of dynamism and renewal. Hence, in the period after the conjuncture of 1979, the incursion of influences such as religious fundamentalism and the neoliberal imperatives of Thatcherism had to a significant extent undermined the modern, secular radicalism that had been built in the previous decades.

In his seminal analysis of the growth of IWAs in the UK, John DeWitt notes how communities of immigrants from the Indian sub-continent had settled in Britain for some decades prior to the arrivals of the 1950s and 1960s. From as early as the 1920s there had been small communities of Indian seamen in port cities and Indian pedlars in the Midlands and the North. While the seamen were mainly Muslims, the pedlars were Bhattra Sikhs, members of an itinerant merchant community from the Punjab.[28] DeWitt recounts a meeting in the course of his research with quite possibly the first Sikh settler to arrive in Southall:

> I met a man who had lived in Southall…since 1936. He was an ordinary villager who had little education, no English, and came from a family with too many sons and not enough land. After a time in England he saved enough money to buy a house in Southall, since when dozens of men from his village have come to England through him; he provided them with food until they found a job and with lodgings until they decided to buy their own houses.[29]

Such a pattern of settlement and support continued into the postwar period. Writing of the mid 1960s, prior to the arrival of Asians from Kenya (1967) and Uganda (1972), Dewitt notes how practically all of the postwar immigrants from India had come from areas in the states of Punjab and Gujarat. Of the predominantly Sikh Punjabis, the bulk of immigrants had come from the Jullundur and Hoshiarpur districts in the heart of the state, often the younger sons of their families, prompted by rural overpopulation at home and the promise of higher wages abroad to make the journey west.[30] Hence, in the early 1950s the majority of Southall's Asian workers were of rural-peasant origins with a steady trickle of white collar workers such as teachers and clerks,[31] a decade or so of migration that was definitively checked by the tightening of immigration controls from the early 1960s.

From the late 1940s, the first social and political networks to arise were those of single men, the widespread practice of arranging for the passage of spouses and children from India being as yet to come. These men would often be known to one another from their local area, or *Ilaqa*, in the Punjab. Yet two factors soon contributed to the erosion of *Ilaqa* ties and the growth of a distinct sense of belonging to Southall's Asian community: the arrival of spouses and children, and the solidarity promoted between men by factory work. Settling into a routine of family life with wives and children, Asian men often spent less time in the *Ilaqa*-based boarding houses and drinking circles that they had previously frequented. At the same time, the men met and befriended other Asians in the course of factory work, often building trust in the course of industrial struggles overseen by the local IWA.[32]

The IWAs and their sister organisations of Pakistani workers that grew up in Asian communities throughout Britain in the 1950s were vital to their members in satisfying the dual functions, along with religious organisations, of being an integral component of growing public spheres, and central representatives of the interests of Asian workers in relation to employers and trade unions alike. The IWAs of the 1950s were actually the 'second wave' of such organisations, the first of their wartime predecessors being formed in Coventry in 1938 from among the Punjabi pedlars and factory workers of the area. Yet these early organisations generally declined with the satisfaction of their central *raison d'être*: the independence won by India from the British in 1947.[33] The importance granted to Indian issues relative to those affecting the Asian community in the UK would decline to a general parity with the second and third 'waves' of organisation of the postwar IWAs and the groupings of second-generation Asians.

Attracted by the plenitude of unskilled, often monotonous and dirty, work offered in the Southall area by firms such as Woolf's Rubber Company and

Krafts, and unhampered by the as yet undiscriminating immigration system, a significant number of first-generation Asians arrived in Southall in the 1950s. By the end of the decade a vibrant public sphere had already begun to arise with the formation of the Southall IWA in 1957 and the first Sikh temple, or *Gurdwara*, in 1959.[34] These institutions complemented the community fora that had already grown up around meetings in Southall Park, local pubs and private homes.[35]

Yet the very rapidity of development of Asian public spheres in Britain in comparison with the bourgeois and working-class examples mentioned earlier can be explained by two factors unique to settings such as Southall: their distinct territorial delimitation and their particularly intense stimulation by, and emission of, flows of communication.

The territorial constitution of communities such as Southall has generally been due, on the one hand, to the solidarity and support facilitated by cultural and language ties, and, on the other, to being pushed together by 'default' by the shared experience of racism. Southall was particularly illustrative of the second territorialisation of the public sphere due to discrimination initially experienced in the realm of housing. An early problem for Asians in Southall was the experience of overcrowding:[36] the pressure to be near sources of work, the expense involved in house buying and the commonplace reluctance of white residents to rent to Black and Asian tenants, all conspired to create the situation of excessive numbers of male residents sharing rooms in overcrowded boarding houses. This practice was rapidly exploited by racists such as the British National Party (BNP) candidate John Bean, who fought in the 1963 local election in Southall, and the antagonistic white locals who formed the Southall Residents Association (SRA) in the same year, the latter describing the very presence of Asian residents as a 'health hazard'.[37] Yet, at the same time, the association[38] actually used such rhetoric as the justification for pressurising the council to buy vacant houses to prevent Asian residents from buying or renting them, particularly on the fringes of Southall.[39] Participation by the local council in this process of ghettoisation was also expressed by the tendency to neglect the cleaning and maintenance of the built environment, neglect that was further blamed by white residents on the Asian community.[40] The initial territorialisation of Southall's public sphere was also imposed by gangs of racists who menaced Asian residents, particularly at the fringes of the town. Yet, in later years the maintenance of Southall's perimeter would become an expression of defiance and autonomy as militant Asian youth acted to prevent incursions by racists, and hence to protect the integrity of the area.

In a seminal discussion of the causal 'flows' of influence and communication that typically enrich and issue forth from heterogeneous, particularly multicultural, public spheres, Arjun Appadurai encourages a movement beyond the binary reductionism of centre/periphery or deterministic/vulgar Marxian accounts in favour of a more plural approach. Appadurai posits the mutually symbiotic relationship between five types of global cultural flow —each exhibiting a particular combination of base and superstructural features—that act upon each other in unpredictable ways, contributing to the dynamism and fertility of public spheres such as Southall that are formed by them: ethnoscapes, mediascapes, technoscapes, financescapes and ideoscapes.[41]

Of these, ethnoscapes are perhaps the most obviously associated with Southall in being composed of the persons and cultures of successive waves of immigrant worker and refugee from the developing world, whether Punjabi, East African or, increasingly in the 1990s, Somalian. The importance of letter writing between relatives in the UK and the subcontinent to the maintenance of such ethnoscapes cannot be understated.[42]

From the organisation of film shows by the IWAs in the late 1950s, and the subsequent opening of the Indian cinemas, to the proliferation of pirate video tapes of recent releases in the 1980s, the incursion of Bollywood cinema, along with that of film and popular Hindi music and its supporting literature of magazines, have constituted a significant mediascape impacting on the lives of those in Southall.

As noted previously, the novelty of Appadurai's flows lies in their mutual reflexivity, and particularly in the extent to which influence flows back and forth between Western and Asian contexts in turn. Hence, with a broad definition that encompasses processes of multinational investment and manufacture, the notion of a technoscape might be illustrated by the instance of politico-economic pressures applied from Southall impacting on investment patterns in India. Hence, outraged at the racist murder in 1976 of Gurdip Singh Chaggar and faced with the general indifference of a Labour administration concerned to maintain working-class support, Asian leaders in Southall threatened to press for the nationalisation of British-owned interests in India if prime minister Callaghan were to refuse an invitation to walk at the head of the funeral cortege of the murdered youngster.[43] The ultimate futility of the gesture aside, such actions were indicative of the increasing awareness among Southall Asians of their capacity to influence the subcontinent. The existence of financescapes based on the practice of sending money to relatives had, of course, been an early expression of this capacity to economically influence events 'at home'.

Finally, ideoscapes too have, from their inception, been subject to a two-way flow between Southall and India. Western political ideologies, such as socialism and communism, enjoyed significant adherence in India in the postwar period. As a result, it was common for IWA politics across the UK to be bifurcated between rival communist and non-communist groupings, with nuclei of members in the local CPGB and independent groupings (often centred around *Gurdwara, Ilaqa* or business networks) respectively.[44] Indeed, successive splits within the Indian CP (CPI), leading in turn to the breakaway Communist Party of India Marxist (CPM) and the Maoist-inspired Communist Party of India Marxist-Leninist (CPML), were to a certain extent paralleled by communist factionalism in the IWAs.[45] Similarly, anti-colonial traditions of resistance from the subcontinent, whether Gandhian or otherwise, had for both first and second generations been a common source of inspiration for mobilisations in Southall, such as in the rallies against British policies toward Rhodesia and the Vietnam War.[46] DeWitt provides a further example of the circular flow of ideoscapes when he describes how dedicated members of the CPGB from Southall would often raise funds, and urge their relatives at home to vote and canvass for the CPI and CPM, thereby seeking to influence events at home.[47] Such practices would resurface in the 1980s in the service of militant Sikh demands for an independent state of Khalistan.

Ultimately, the combination of territorial concentration and intense stimulation by manifold communicational flows can be sited as the source of the rapidity with which Southall's public sphere developed. To a certain extent this public sphere constituted an independently evolving 'continuum' between the UK and the subcontinent, an 'imagined world'[48] with a distinct phenomenology and ontology formed at the intersection between the flows from each of these two locales, yet peculiarly independent of each. Taking the example of ideoscapes, DeWitt notes how in the 1950s and 1960s the CPGB was inundated with Asian members, a few of whom were previously members of the Communist Party of India while the majority were apolitical and joined only to gain influence in the local IWAs. The result, compounded by language problems, was the formation of parallel CPGB branches where meetings were focussed exclusively on South Asian and IWA politics rather than issues in the UK.[49] This concern with an exclusively Southall-India continuum was, however, expanded by second-generation Asians concerned to demonstrate their right to acceptance and equality in British society into a more inclusive and developed UK-India continuum. Southall has thus constituted an evolving zone, one that reached a fleetingly autonomous and modern form of life in the wake of the conjuncture of

1979, only to succumb to less progressive influences such as fundamentalism and Thatcherism in the 1980s.

Paul Gilroy develops a compelling account of NSMs as forms of progressive, urban political organisation that have developed among ethnic minority groups in place of otherwise narrow working-class movements which take labour and its emancipation from capitalist servitude as their central aim and source of identity.[50] NSMs have a distinct set of goals such as control over collective consumption, cultural identity and political autonomy that set them apart from socialist concerns such as the conquest of state power.[51] I will continue this section by arguing that the NSMs of Southall's residents actually represented the reified expression of the community public sphere's political will in the form of loose, modern and unhierarchical organisations. In this respect, Southall's IWA, with the participation in industrial disputes as one of its central roles, actually straddles the role of an 'old', labourist and 'new' social movement. Indeed, the growth of community-based industrial action to fill the void left by trade union indifference was more general than merely that of the IWA, encompassing the extension of credit and the donation of free food from shopkeepers, the waiving of rent for weeks at a time by landlords, and the collections made by the *Gurdwara* on behalf of strikers, acts that resembled the support given by villages in rural Punjab to their striking kin in nearby industrial centres.[52] Second-generation organisations such as the SYM, Peoples Unite, SMG and SBS represent the culmination of this process, particularly in their experimentation with post-traditional forms of life, identity and organisation.[53]

The year 1965 was a politically significant one for Southall with the local IWA playing a central role in the life of the public sphere and, to a lesser extent, showing signs of itself being, through certain of its factions along with individuals and groups such as the CPGB, an early, still significantly labour-orientated, NSM.

In the first case, Southall in 1965 was the location of probably the single most impressive, in sheer volume of participation, of the IWA's bi-annual election campaigns that Britain's Asian communities had ever seen. Preparations by rival groups had been in progress for some months prior to the events until five slates and a number of independent candidates emerged each holding rallies and distributing dozens of manifestos. In all, perhaps a hundred men took time off work to participate in the canvassing effort and a total of 3,000 Asians voted, a number constituting about half of the adult male population of Southall and surrounding areas.[54]

Yet, along with the aforementioned development of Southall's public sphere, 1965 would also be remembered as an early and decisive test of the community's political solidarity and assertion in dealings with local employers and trade unions and thus, as a promising step on the road toward the autonomist aspirations of an NSM. Though Britain's trade unions had perhaps more contact with Asians, both as individuals and as members of IWAs, than any other large institution,[55] their feelings toward ethnic workers such as those of Southall had evolved from an initial indifference in the early 1950s to considerable resentment as the next decade wore on.[56] Henry Pelling's otherwise competent study of British trade unionism itself exemplifies the unease and indifference of unions at the time toward the issue of race, with only two pages of the book allotted to this issue, and then to offering a defence of the unions as allayers of popular fears of cheap foreign labour. Pelling continues in this union-friendly vein with the assertion that individuals and not the majority of the membership were to blame for xenophobic attitudes and that the lack of Asian recruitment by unions was merely a sin of 'omission' rather than of 'commission'.[57] Sadly, the experience of Southall's workers was far from resembling Pelling's account.

By 1965, 90 per cent of the unskilled workers at Woolf's Rubber Company in Southall were Punjabi. Indeed, the requirement for cheap, unskilled labour to work there had been the main reason for the large-scale settlement of Asian workers and subsequent ethnic composition of the town in later years. The factory made rubber accessories for prams and the motor industry, production that involved the use of sulphur and carbon black. Hence, alongside the low wages and common working week of 60 hours, conditions at the factory for the Asian workers were hard.

Despite the vehemently anti-union stance of the family owners of Woolf's, attempts to organise the workforce had been made in 1958 by the Amalgamated Engineering Union and in 1960 by the Transport and General Workers' Union (TGWU). Yet these initial attempts failed and the organisers were sacked, their efforts hampered in no small part by the attitude of white workers not keen to join a 'black' union branch,[58] and by the fact that several of the influential 'touts' at the factory who commonly demanded bribes from fellow Asian workers for hiring and overtime-related issues were Punjabis involved in IWA politics, one actually sitting on the IWA executive committee.[59]

In light of the latter case of IWA loyalties being divided between radicalism and the Woolf's status quo, DeWitt contests the popular account of the third, successful, recruitment drive of 1963 that attributed its eventual success entirely to the IWA.[60] Rather, in the wake of failures at political mobilisation through the trade union movement, the people of Southall began to organise their efforts on a community basis, and only partially through the IWA. In fact, the initial impetus came from two Punjabi members of the CPGB who worked at the factory rather than being official IWA policy. Encouraged by their fellow Punjabi comrades and introduced to trade union representatives by the local party secretary, the two Punjabi CPers visited the Southall branch of the TGWU accompanied by two communist members of the IWA executive committee.[61] Ultimately two factors in the Woolf's episode have to be taken into account: (a) the IWA was not monolithic, its factions split along the same kinds of radical and conservative lines as the rest of the community so that its evolution into an NSM was to a certain extent stymied from within; and (b) the importance of the CPGB and other left-wing groups in the Woolf's strike and subsequent Southall history cannot be underestimated, continuing as they did to influence the town's public sphere and NSMs until the conjuncture of 1979.

In 1963 members of the IWA executive, including communists employed at the factory, used their position to recruit intensively for the TGWU outside of the actual shop floor by going from door to door and holding community meetings. As a result of these actions, the previously widespread practice of having to bribe foremen to get and keep jobs and overtime ended and the factory won union recognition in 1964. Yet a number of unjustified sackings from 1964–5 which were greeted with indifference and inaction by the union forced the workers to come out on strike. The TGWU's initial reaction was confused, pledges of support being made yet accompanied by no strike pay, while TGWU-controlled lorries were permitted to cross the picket line. The management also sought to undermine the strike by trying to recruit Pakistani workers from as far away as Bradford, actions that prompted the IWA and Pakistani Workers Association leaders to intervene. As mentioned, community efforts indicative of the growth of a NSM included the extension of credit from shopkeepers, the landlords waiving rent for a few weeks and a collection of £1500 to support the strike. Sadly, the strike collapsed after seven weeks, resulting in the sacking of union activists and the downgrading of other workers. The firm itself was so badly affected by the loss of orders that it collapsed the following year.[62]

Ultimately the Woolf's strike, along with successive struggles such as the one at Perivale Gutterman, attained folkloric status, contributing a particular solidarity, militancy and self-confidence to the community that would help to concretise its distinctive public sphere and to fortify the nascent structures of its NSMs.

In terms of the public sphere, Southall's youth continued with the practice of their parents of mixing political and cultural influences from East and West. Yet the combination of these was now more evenly divided between the two spheres, while the 'continuum' formed by Southall came increasingly to resemble an autonomous, hybrid zone uniting progressive currents from the UK and the subcontinent. Always in a dynamic relationship, the balance between these two poles would further shift toward the UK, particularly to the Afro-Caribbean influences found there. An often-painful division between cultures came to be a common experience for youth from Asian communities at the time. Research carried out by the Community Relations Council in 1975 repeatedly illustrated the extent to which, compared with their parents, young Asians were keen to expand their acquaintances with white and Afro-Caribbean youth, to explore unsupervised relationships with the opposite sex, and to experiment with prevalent youth trends and fashions of the day.[63] A dissatisfaction with the political leadership offered by their parents was also a common refrain,[64] a depth of feeling voiced by one Asian youth interviewed in the course of BBC Radio coverage on the day following the violence of 23 April 1979:

> This is our future, right…our leaders will do nothing…our leaders wanted a peaceful sit down, but what can you do with a peaceful sit down here…we had to do something, the young people—we don't want a situation like the East End where our brothers and sisters are being attacked every day…I believe that the youth of Southall have left a trademark…they have shown that the National Front is not welcome here.[65]

Yet the youths interviewed also held views close to their parents on issues such as the eventual desirability of arranged marriage.[66] In the case of Southall, the result of these contradictory pulls was the growth of an exhilaratingly progressive youth culture in areas such as militant anti-racism, demands for police and state accountability, and solidarity with broader left-wing struggles (including those in Northern Ireland), combined with an occasionally stolid illiberalism on issues such gender equality[67] which would be tackled by the 'second wave' of NSMs, SMG and SBS, in the wake of 1979. The former, solidaristic, traditions of the Black left grew steadily in the 1970s, beginning with significant episodes of cooperation between Afro-Caribbean and Asian youth such the assistance given by the former when gangs of skinheads attacked Southall in 1970. Such encounters helped to overcome much of the mutual suspicion that had previously existed between these groups. At the same time, Asian youth drew on Black music such as soul and reggae and on the urban styles and attitudes of young Afro-Caribbeans in crafting more assertive identities for themselves. Hence a fertile, cosmopolitan and radical culture grew in the Southall of the 1970s, helped on its way by interracial community events such as the Rock Against Racism carnival held in 1978.

A corresponding patchwork of interwoven 'myths' was apparent in the wake of the murder of Blair Peach as the traditions of heroic sacrifice held by the white and black defenders of Southall coalesced for a moment, all communities fleetingly united by their grief. The face of the frail, bearded young martyr no doubt coaxed forth images of Christ in the minds of religiously inclined white sympathisers, and succeeded Kevin Gately, who died in a June 1974 demonstration against the NF, as an exemplar of heroic anti-fascism for the secular left. Peach's death also had particular reverence for the predominantly Sikh Punjabi community, both as a white man who chose to assist them and thereby defend their right to reside in the country, and as an enemy of tyrannous oppressors whose struggles with the Sikhs are still talked of and remembered in popular *bazaar* calendar art.[68] Indeed, in the wake of the massive demonstration of 28 April, where a sombre litany of prayer was dedicated to Peach,[69] signifying his admittance to Southall's Sikh congregation through the 'principle of vicariousness' common to its religious martyrs,[70] the words of the Sikh scholar, J.P.S. Uberoi, come to mind:

> The final lesson of martyrdom then, whether one studies it in history, theology or sociology, is that it marks at once the both the limits of power, especially state power, and the limitlessness of self-sacrifice conceived as salvation-in-society.[71]

Formed in the wake of Gurdip Singh Chaggar's murder in 1976, the SYM experienced its political baptism on 23 April 1979. Yet the solidarity of Southall's Asian youths had been growing steadily for some years prior to this event. In particular, traditions such as the practice among the older boys of escorting Asian children home from school in areas where they might otherwise experience racial attack were vital to forging such bonds.[72] Along with Peoples Unite, the SYM had built on the history of secular radicalism present in certain factions of the IWA that had existed since the era of Woolf's. This NSM was also encouraged by the example of its Afro-Caribbean allies to identify itself more fully with urban black protest, thereby helping to overcome the often insular outlook of the older generation.[73]

The year 1976 also saw the opening of Southall Rights, a free legal advice centre which defended many of those arrested on 23 April 1979. The centre was a particularly important addition to the public sphere in the extent to which it contributed a legal dimension to campaigning resources of local NSMs.

Yet the final maturation of Southall's NSMs into distinctly modern, progressive groupings actually came with the 'second wave' groups SMG and

SBS, where the radical spirit was focussed on areas such as domestic violence that were less palatable to traditionalists. Sadly, though SMG and SBS have maintained these elevated traditions to the present day, the era after the conjuncture of 1979 would see the ascendancy of very different currents, in particular those of fundamentalisms perhaps more virulent than among even the most devout members of the first generation.

Gita Sahgal of SBS notes how the separatist calls for Khalistan, a theocratic Sikh homeland in the Punjab, in the early 1980s were emblematic of this turn to fundamentalism. Indeed, with the relative decline of the NF after the election of 1979, calls for Khalistan became the rallying cry for much of the youth that had comprised the rump of the SYM and, increasingly, the criminal fraternities of Southall's gangs. Sahgal points out how fundamentalists were united in their espousal of romantic and utopian forms of anti-modernism, often expressed in calls to scale back the secularist achievements of organisations in Southall such as the autonomy for women championed by SBS. In part, notes Sahgal, the fundamentalist 'turn' had been encouraged by the negligence of multiculturalists toward the illiberalism present in many traditional Asian worldviews, an omission that had allowed conservative community leaders the freedom to cultivate fiefdoms such as Southall by occupying a 'neo-colonial' comprador role in relation to the local authorities.[74] Over-caution on the part of multiculturalists had also resulted in the inability to challenge the spread of gang violence among Southall's youth through fears of replicating the kinds of racism shown by the police towards them.[75]

Ultimately, Southall's fundamentalist turn also poses problems for the model of NSMs put forward by Gilroy. Noting the decline of secular strands of socialist organisation, and foregrounding the eurocentrism and exclusivity commonly displayed in its dealings with ethnic minority communities, Gilroy welcomes the rise of the concept of race as a mobilising category to replace class among NSMs, encouraging the emulation of feudal movements that sought to resist the onset of capitalist modernisation.[76] Yet such a perspective risks encouraging precisely the fundamentalist forces mentioned by Sahgal, while at the same time neglecting the centrality of socialist, not to mention communist, contributions to the rise of the most progressive resistance traditions of communities such as Southall. Gilroy appears to present the choice between the forms of 'Utopian democratic populism' traditionally employed in communities such as Southall, and exclusively ethnic formations, as simply a pragmatic substitution of new for redundant old inspirations.[77] Such a casual dismissal of secular radicalism can, as the case of Southall shows, have worrying ramifications.

Southall and the British left

Setting aside the pre-1947 cooperation between IWAs and sections of the left in calling for an end to British rule in India, two distinct stages of interaction between members of Asian communities such as Southall and the left can be identified: that of the first generation's liaisons with, predominantly Stalinist, groupings such as the CPGB; and the more active engagement of second-generation Asians with their peers in the post-1968 New Left.

As mentioned in the previous section, the widespread sense of separateness felt by first-generation Asians toward British institutions, promoted partly by their commonly held expectation of return to the subcontinent once they had saved sufficient funds, was matched by a corresponding sense of bewilderment, and hence neglect of them, by the British left. Homi Bhabha suggests a continuum between such 'benign', essentially sympathetic, forms of neglect and more 'malign' ones when he distinguishes between a 'large trade union internationalism' and an 'ethnocentric little Englandism'[78] as the two attitudes of the old left toward the subject of race.

The former tendency was exemplified by the openness of the CPGB to parallel Asian branch meetings based on the attitude, shared by the Asians themselves, of an inherent separateness of concerns and probability of return to the subcontinent that militated against the need for integration.

More malign expressions of neglect and even hostility were confined mainly to those on the right of the Labour Party, such as Bob Mellish, who were particularly enamoured of Powell's opposition to New Commonwealth immigration and membership of the European Community.[79] Pargiter's sedulous courtship of the Punjabi vote on behalf of Labour during the 1964 election campaign, only to ignore and castigate his benefactors as an expression of solidarity with white residents in the wake of victory, evidenced a similar mentality in the case of Southall.[80] Perhaps the most disturbing expression of these sentiments arose in the late 1960s with the sporadic, yet increasingly common, activism among trade unionists in favour of Powell's views, from the solidarity marches of the London dockers and Smithfield meat porters in 1968 to the protests by white workers in Southall in the same year.[81] Such activities were maintained to a certain extent by the activism of a few cells of 'Strasserite' NF activists within certain quarters of the trade union movement, their success prompting them to form the short-lived breakaway National Party (NP) in 1976. Taking their inspiration from the opposition to Hitler among 'left leaning' Nazis such as Otto Strasser, this group combined syndicalist economic radicalism with populist ultranationalism.[82]

The attitude of the union leadership tended to reside at the centre of Bhabha's continuum, with a general indifference to New Commonwealth immigration in the 1950s giving way to selectively discriminatory utterances and actions in the hope of placating the working-class membership.[83]

Levels of cooperation between second-generation Asians and members of the heterogeneous, often Trotskyite, New Left were, perhaps unsurprisingly, greater than that of their predecessors. In part, this was undoubtedly due to the greater radicalism and internationalism of the New Left (and in no way inhibited by the latter's relative absence of working-class membership). Yet perhaps the most obvious reason was the awareness among Asian youths that they would not be making the return journey dreamt of by their parents and hence, that they would have to directly contest the racist aggression that had previously been suffered in silence.

Increasing levels of identification and cooperation in the 1970s between the radical left and Asians in the sphere of industrial action was perhaps most visible in the case of the strike at the Grunwick film processing factory in West London in 1977. Marwick notes how the strike that arose there among predominantly Asian workers became a *cause célèbre* of the left, bringing out not only Trotskyites but members of the mainstream Labour Party and trade union movement.[84] Largely ignored by the trade union mainstream, the dispute was also significant as an instance of the mobilisation of flying pickets, including Yorkshire miners,[85] which had been a common feature of the tense industrial relations of the decade. Indeed, the extent to which the struggles of Asian workers and communities, regarded by sections of the New Left as a domestic extension of the vanguard role assigned to the forces of revolution in the developing world, were becoming a focal point for radicalism at the time was jokingly summed up by one demonstrator who suggested that 'This is the Ascot of the left…it is essential to be seen here and best of all to get arrested'.[86]

Hence in the political climate of the 1970s, black and Asian communities were increasingly looked to as outposts of resistance and recruitment by the radical left. In the case of Southall, which by 1979 had become a 'Mecca' for the West London left, the increasing concentration of activism in the area had a distinct impact on the public sphere which was enriched by the a wide variety of contemporary political and cultural currents from reggae and soul music to Third World Marxism. While poetry and songs from the subcontinent had been employed as means of conveying political ideas from the earliest days of the postwar IWAs.[87] the increasingly hybrid nature of Southall's youth culture was a further sign of the burgeoning cosmopolitanism of its public sphere.

Yet this proximity and cross fertilisation also gave rise to tensions between the young Asians and their left-wing peers. Echoing Gilroy's account of the omissions on the part of the labourist left toward ethnic minority issues that had contributed to the rise of NSMs, Bhabha notes:

> Whenever questions of race and sexuality make their own organisational and theoretical ethical demands on the primacy of 'class', 'state' and 'party' the language of traditional socialism is quick to describe those urgent, 'other' questions as symptoms of petty-bourgeois deviation, signs of the bad faith of socialist intellectuals.[88]

Such tensions were certainly present in the 1970s in the context of the popular front tactics of the ANL which were criticised by many on the Asian left for marginalising anti-racist/imperialist, anti-capitalist and direct action tactics in the hope of retaining the support of moderates, including the Labour Party, for their limited anti-Nazi activities.[89] A founding member of the SYM, Balraj Puriwal, notes how the contributions to street politics in Southall of the SWP and ANL cadres in the 1970s thus affected a 'colonisation' of local initiatives which were thereby undermined:

> I personally in the SYM did not know at the start what moderate or far left meant…we had the ANL and SWP but I felt they were talking a language of politics I didn't relate to…even now I don't know what left and right in Southall means. Every time we tried to protest and give our own identity the left tried to take it over…they gave us their slogans and placards…our own identity was subsumed, diffused and deflected all over the place. They collectively undermined our development…the SYM and IWA struggled to keep their own identity.[90]

The tensions documented above are similar to those touched upon in the previous section. They arise from the need to maintain the delicate equilibrium between the progressive influences of secular, particularly socialistic, modernity, and the reservoir of identity and symbolic reproduction drawn on by the community from its traditional culture. The balance achieved between these tendencies, such as in April 1979 or, more enduringly, through the legacy of 'second wave' NSMs such as SMG, is ultimately vulnerable to the ascendancy of either one, whether that of takeover by the socialist left, or attack from the forces of fundamentalism. Sadly, the conjuncture of 23 April 1979, alongside the uprising of 1981 that culminated in the burning of the Hambrough Tavern, evidenced perhaps the last, large-scale mobilisations based on the complementary interaction between the two forces.

Race, the New Right and elite power

A series of fifteen sombre photographs from the disturbances of 23 April 1979 and the march of 28 April form a short lacuna in the text of the NCCL report. Each of them offers a window into different episodes of the momentous two days in the history of Southall. Yet, on closer inspection, photograph number three is marked by a deeper imprint of the times, displaying in its peripheral details the marks of the zeitgeist that Walter Benjamin might have identified as a historical 'configuration pregnant with tensions', a 'monad' on which the manifold conflicts and injustices of the era were inscribed. A hundred or so demonstrators, mainly Asians and a few Afro-Caribbeans, are congregated at a junction a few hundred metres from the town hall. It is 5 pm, a couple of hours before the escalation of tensions and police aggression that are to follow. The scene appears good natured, with demonstrators and even a policeman smiling as steward Clarence Baker requests through a megaphone that protesters remain on the pavement. Yet one of the three billboards in the background offers a portent of the streams of causation that had been building over the previous decades, soon to reach a point of climax with the Conservative victory in the general election a few weeks from then. 'Labour Still Isn't Working' reads the title to the advert, while underneath, against a blank white background, an unemployment queue recedes into the distance. The juxtaposition of this poster and the crowds of demonstrators below together foreground the themes that will be explored in the following section: the poster proclaims an end to the era of Labour and trade union hegemony that had begun in 1964; the launch of a 'New Right' politics that would 'work' where labourism did not hints at the ascendancy of neoliberal elites to come; the marshalling of a range of political, intellectual and, as the Saatchi and Saatchi poster itself exemplified, media resources in the service of elite power that had momentarily been wrong-footed by the popular protest of the 1960s; the perceived need for greater public order in the wake of such protest; and the centrality of race to this new political vanguard.

The radical protest and counter-cultures of the 1960s had been a significant source of concern to Western elites throughout the decade. A common refrain from establishment critiques was that these movements were evidence of the essential 'ungovernability' brought on as central institutions of governance were increasingly being overloaded by an unreasonably demanding and troublesome public. Hence protest, alongside other 'crisis phenomena' such as rising crime, was presented as an expression of the multiplying wants and rights that an egoistic public was confronting its government with, overburdening the machinery of the Keynesian state administrative apparatus as a result. The blame for the crises was not levelled at the more deserving target of the economy and state administration themselves[91] which, by the 1970s, were experiencing the disruptive influence of the energy crisis.

From the 1960s, a concerted effort by the inchoate New Right to contest the gains made both by radicals and reformists was initiated on three mutually reinforcing fronts: the mobilisation of intellectual, media and ideological resources against the protest movements and their perceived allies in the Keynesian state administration under the encompassing banner of anti-communism; the promotion of monetarist, laissez-faire policies in the economic sphere; and the neo-authoritarian militarisation of the police force as the means of defending the aforementioned policies from opponents on the left. Indeed, the mobilisation of police forces would be a central means by which forces critical of the New Right project such as trade unions were to be broken up and their members disciplined. Perhaps the first, large-scale, implementation of these policies was to be seen in Chile where the American-backed coup by General Pinochet against the democratically elected government of Salvador Allende led swiftly to the implementation of economic policies based on the monetarist prescriptions of the Chicago school.

Blumenthal notes of this movement in the United States which culminated in the Reagan administration, that the radical right sought to undermine the 'Liberal Establishment' through channels such as think tanks and greater prominence in the press.[92] William Simon, treasury secretary under president Ford, also exemplified this tendency with his calls for the formation of a 'counter-intelligentsia' to attack America's perceived East Coast 'liberal fortress'.[93] Ultimately, notes Blumenthal,

> [t]o counteract this Liberal Establishment, which conservatives believed encompassed both political parties, they deliberately created the Counter-Establishment. By constructing their own establishment, piece by piece, they hoped to supplant the liberals. Their version of Brookings [the liberal US think tank] would be bigger and better...The editorial pages of the *Wall Street Journal* would set the agenda with more prescience than *The New York Times*.[94]

A similar remarshalling of beleaguered elites by the New Right, in this case evolving from the Powellite elitism of the 1960s into the populism of the Thatcher era, occurred in the UK in the fertile environment of the energy crisis: the decade of the 'oil shocks' would offer numerous instances of crisis phenomena which, in light of their often remote causation by distant and abstract processes in the global economy, could conveniently be blamed on scapegoats such as Southall's Asian community.

A significant juncture in this process was the setting up in 1974, the year when the industrial and racial conflict symptomatic of the 'ungovernability thesis' brought down the Heath government, of the monetarist, anti-collectivist Centre for Policy Studies by Margaret Thatcher and former cabinet minister Sir Keith Joseph.[95] The cultivation of leading right-wing journalists and intellectuals was a central plank in this project with considerable cross-fertilisation of ideas and even personnel occurring between the think tanks and learned journals, the broadsheet newspapers and the tabloids, the latter receiving their broadly Powellite brief from the more 'elevated' agenda setters. A favoured theme of these publications, once again indebted to Powell's paranoid theses, was that of the left, anti-racists and immigrant communities as a 'dangerous minority' of 'enemies within' who threatened to undermine the British state and society.[96]

The subject of race was a constant point of reference for the forces of the New Right. Indeed, the peculiar combination of authoritarianism, anti-immigration rhetoric and *laissez-faire* economics that had been espoused throughout the 1960s by agenda setters such as Enoch Powell, and even in right-wing Labour Party circles, would prove to be a potent weapon against the left in years to come.[97] The saliency of race in the public mind had actually been increasing since the 1950s when disturbances such as those of 1958 in Notting Hill began to receive attention in the media,[98] developments prompting Marwick to suggest that by the time of the 1974 election race had become the single most significant cleavage in British politics, outdoing even class in importance.[99] Perhaps paradoxically, the mass politicisation of race coincided with the era of Labour Party and trade union hegemony that lasted from approximately the Labour election victory of 1964 to the defeat of 1979. The first conspicuous signpost of this era was the imposition of controls on immigration from the New Commonwealth in 1962 in the face of mounting public pressure, a trend that has continued unabated to the present day. Prior to this, a universal open door policy had operated from 1948 with regard to Commonwealth immigration, a policy maintained due to an attachment to Old, rather than New, Commonwealth entrants, and which was reluctantly curtailed only due to the public, and often elite, aversion to the latter.[100]

The election in 1964 of a Conservative candidate in the safe Labour seat of Smethwick, which proved an exception to the otherwise leftward swing of the day, was the second decisive sign of the turbulent times to come. Perhaps best remembered for the frequently misquoted remarks of children in the municipal elections of 1963, whose claims that 'If you want a nigger for a neighbour, vote Labour' were tacitly condoned by the Conservative candidate,[101] the outcome of Smethwick in 1964 sent shockwaves through the

Labour and the trade union movement,[102] heralding their nervousness and vacillation toward issues of race in years to come. Yet, as mentioned previously, perhaps the single most significant contribution to the 'racialisation' of political debate came with Enoch Powell's 'rivers of blood' speech in 1968 which, notes Suresh Grover, changed the political atmosphere 'overnight', providing the catalyst to the rapid success of the far right in the early 1970s and the era of 'paki bashing' inaugurated by it.[103]

Powell was significant in the extent to which he personified the intersection of xenophobic and authoritarian nationalism, and liberal economics that characterised much of the New Right project in Britain. As a tendency within the Conservative Party, this movement also regarded the liberalism of Heathite Toryism, rather than merely the left, as contributing to the problems of the early 1970s captured under the umbrella of the 'ungovernability thesis'. More turbulent than the Winter of Discontent that would form the context of the disturbances in Southall of 1979, the era of ungovernability, roughly taken to coincide with the Heath government's term in office, saw the intersection of a number of distinct crisis tendencies. The wildcat strikes of the 1960s were replaced by mass industrial action, instigated to a significant extent by the radical left operating in the trade union movement, in which 'flying pickets' were commonly employed and which were characterised by worrying levels of violence and intimidation from both strikers and the police. Ultimately, trade union militancy culminated in the miners' strike of 1973–4 which brought down the Heath government, hence stymieing its attempts to control industrial violence through the Industrial Relations Act of 1971. The same unions would be bound in the next decade by the stricter legislation of the Thatcher era. Draconian legislation was also prompted by the IRA bomb attacks of 1974 in which twenty-nine people were killed and more than two hundred badly injured, leading to the Prevention of Terrorism Act in the same year. Hence, unsurprisingly, crisis tendencies had contributed to the increasing levels of state surveillance, control and militarisation against the public called for by the New Right.

Black communities, already menaced by racist violence at the time, were a particular target for new styles of policing whose development had been informed by the anxieties of the ungovernability thesis, making them the unfortunate inheritors of much of the New Right project. A central component of police strategy was the belief in the need to prevent conflict before it occurred, a change in emphasis from traditional concerns with 'law and order' to those of 'public order'.[104] Hence conciliatory innovations such as community policing and draconian, 'neo-colonial'[105] approaches of forces such as the SPG were united in having originated from the desire to extend state control and surveillance into the everyday lives of citizens. At the core of these initiatives was the elision of crime with any sort of public protest,[106] policies that would result in police violence, mass arrests and criminalisation of a whole community when the people of Southall attempted to protest at the provocations of the NF on 23 April 1979.

By the time of the Winter of Discontent, of which the 'Southall Riots' formed an integral episode, the manifold contingencies that would culminate in Thatcher's election victory were on the verge of fruition. Although actual instability had declined since the era of the ungovernability thesis, January 1979 saw more workers out on strike than since the General Strike of 1926,[107] prompting Marwick to note that

> [t]he situation was not nearly as bad as that of 1974, but in the inventive stories of the right-wing press it sounded bad, on television it looked bad, and for the millions of discomfited citizens it felt bad.[108]

Media coverage of events in Southall was similarly informed by the presuppositions of New Right ideology. Setting aside the unanimous condemnation of the demonstrators and the unreserved praise for the police, a number of other familiar Powellite themes were apparent. Anti-fascist demonstrators were presented as extremists little different to the NF against whom they had come to protest. The overwhelming picture presented was of outsiders coming to the town to make trouble, an account that obscured the largely home-grown mobilisations of the community on the day. Similarly, interviews with participants were concentrated on the members of the ANL and SWP, while community representatives were almost completely ignored. The extent of this denial of any autonomous political agency among the citizens and organisations of Southall was captured in a *Daily Telegraph* cartoon. Depicting a three-tier platform of the sort mounted by athletes at Olympic medal presentation ceremonies, a triumphant member of the NF occupies the top level, while injured members of the ANL and the police force occupy second and third place respectively.[109] In no sense does the image convey the fact that Southall's Asian community were the worst affected of all. Ultimately, it would fall to television coverage to unwittingly offer a more balanced picture: while commentaries on the events followed a predictably establishment line, the actual footage indicated the extent of the police violence and its impact on local people.[110]

Southall and British fascism

Contemporary television footage of the 1979 election meeting in Southall shows a trickle of NF supporters arriving at the town hall, a morbid procession that pauses fleetingly at the entrance to shake their fists, shout insults and offer truculent looks to the small group of demonstrators that had managed to assemble outside a shop across the road. Despite the conspicuous absence of a skinhead contingent on the screen, those in attendance were typical of the third generation of British fascists mobilised by the NF in the late 1970s, groups of predominantly working-class young men whose party would face oblivion in the wake of the 1979 election. Hence, as for the people of Southall, the British left, and the remarshalled New Right, 23 April of that year would also be a moment of conflict followed by a definitive change of fortunes for the far right. Indeed, though the encounter of the fascists with Southall in 1979, and again in 1981, could in no sense be regarded as a *causal* factor in their eventual decline, which had actually begun in the wake of the Heath government's collapse, it can in retrospect be taken as symbolic of the changing zeitgeist, a monad encapsulating the conflicts of the age before their imminent dissolution.

The tortuous history of British fascism in the twentieth century, from its origins amongst groupings of monarchist, imperialist and conservative ultras, through its dalliances with Mussolini and National Socialism, to its final incarnation in the NF, is particularly difficult to chart as its subject matter are numerous obscure, short-lived and often mutually antagonistic sects with rapidly fluctuating memberships. Nevertheless, three distinct tendencies had endured since the interwar years as the inspiration for the second- and third-generation activists of the 1970s: the legacies of Oswald Mosley, Arnold Leese and A.K. Chesterton.[111]

Mosley began his parliamentary career in 1918 as a Conservative MP, yet his idiosyncratic election programme of 'socialistic imperialism' already hinted at the volatile combination of economic radicalism, social Darwinism, eurocentrism, and militarism that would see him crossing the floor to join the Labour Party in 1924, only to subsequently form his own movement in the early 1930s. Though his abiding concern to alleviate unemployment led him to an early interest in the works of Keynes, Hobson and a number of Independent Labour Party figures, he grew increasingly enamoured of the anti-democratic, corporativist[112] principles of Italian fascism, forming his own British Union of Fascists (BUF) in 1932 with substantial assistance from Mussolini himself.[113] At the outset, Mosley fashioned a vitalistic 'culturalist' perspective based on Lamarckian evolutionary theories and Spengler's morphology of cultures, which emphasised culture rather than biological origins as the basis of his political prescriptions.[114] Yet, in common with the influence of Nazism on his hero Mussolini, Mosley would progress from his initial elitism to racism and anti-Semitism of the most virulent kinds in the later 1930s. After his wartime imprisonment, Mosley formed the Union Movement, a grouping that played down its earlier fascist rhetoric, to meet with some initial success in its campaigns against East European and, particularly in Brixton and Notting Hill, West Indian immigrants.[115] Yet Mosley's grandiose plans for a unified fascist Europe under the command of a single party (ironic given the rapid growth of the EC at the time) were radically out of step with the British public, and he passed into relative obscurity in the increasingly xenophobic atmosphere of the 1960s, although his organisational and oratorical styles, and personal example would have an indelible impact on the 'second generation' of fascists, particularly John Tyndall.

Arnold Leese's political career was in many ways the opposite to that of Mosley: although his Imperial Fascist League was at the fringe of British politics in the 1930s, his fanatical anti-Semitism, racism and penchant for conspiracy theories and violent paramilitary tactics were to have more of an influence than Mosley on second-generation fascists in the postwar period. In particular, Leese's Hitler-worshipping disciple Colin Jordan was to be a leading figure in a number of the groups antecedent to the NF and in the British Movement contemporary with it.[116]

A scion of the establishment like Mosley and a leading member of the BUF, A.K. Chesterton, second cousin of writer and anti-Semite G.K. Chesterton,[117] was evidence of the extent to which fascist ideas and support merged into the Conservative mainstream. Though fractionally more moderate than Leese, Chesterton was to have the most direct influence on the second generation fascists through his League of Empire Loyalists, of which Colin Jordan, John Bean, John Tyndall and Martin Webster were members in the 1950s.[118] Yet, it was as the founder of the NF in 1967 that Chesterton would crown his achievements: a muddy fusion of the League of Empire Loyalists and the BNP, along with individual members of the Racial Preservation Societies and Greater Britain Movement (including its founders, Tyndall and Webster), the NF could be viewed as the final synthesis of Mosley's mass politics and economic programme, Leese's anti-Semitism and racial populism, Chesterton's sentimental imperialism, and the further shores of native conservatism.[119]

Yet the finer ideological distinctions between second-generation followers of the three tendencies were of little interest to the public, who were exclusively concerned with halting non-white immigration.[120] The network of local Racial Preservation Societies to which the SRA was affiliated, that grew up in the 1960s to press for such aims, was the organic expression of this largely apolitical racist foment. Hence, popular opposition to New Commonwealth immigration along with Powell's incendiary outbursts provided a fertile environment for the growth of the NF in the late 1960s, while the liberalism of the Heath government and the Ugandan Asian crisis helped membership to reach its peak at around 17,500 in 1972.[121]

The fascist heyday of the early 1970s was important in two other respects: instances of 'paki bashing' became increasingly prevalent at the time, and sympathy, as well as direct support, from bastions of Toryism such as the Monday Club[122] also increased. Indeed, the movement's decline began soon after Thatcher acceded to leadership of the Conservative Party in 1975 and proceeded to coax recalcitrant Tories back into the fold with her own anti-immigration rhetoric. At the same time, a rift between the populist conservatives in the movement and the more openly fascistic elements under Tyndall and Webster weakened the NF further, many of the former defecting to the smaller Strasserite NP.[123] These internal tensions would have a significant impact on the orientations of the movement as a whole. In particular, the violent street politics of the British Movement would have an increasing influence on the National Front with the waning of its conservative and 'left' wings, especially with the elitist Tyndall's ejection in the wake of the 1979 elections and the corresponding ascendancy of pro-skinhead Webster.[124]

Alongside the Tory swing to the right, Thurlow identifies anti-fascist/racist militancy and state surveillance as the main causes of the NF's decline after the conjuncture of 1979.[125] Yet for the residents of Southall, perhaps no keener image of fascist defeat exists than that of the burning Hambrough Tavern of 1981, a Bastille-like symbol of oppression that had finally been overcome.

Conclusion

Rather than accepting the linear, dynamic accounts of history from 'above' that were commonly espoused by his historicist contemporaries, Benjamin sought to freeze time in order to reflect upon the meaning of the apposite moment or detail. Such a fragment, rescued from the relentlessly blowing winds of history, might then be looked to by the historian as a means of empathising with, perhaps even redeeming, the memory of the nameless multitudes otherwise swept away by the 'storm of progress'.[126] It has been the attempt to practise this unorthodox method that has given this paper its peculiar structure and style. Indeed, without Benjamin's example and a long obsession with the 'meaning' of 23 April 1979 on the part of the author, there would scarcely have been a rationale for pulling together the disparate themes of the preceding pages. Hence the essay itself endures as a monad, a point of intersection and conjuncture where time can be made to stand still so that the people of Southall can finally take their place as makers of, and not bystanders to, the drama of the 1970s.

Notes

1. This article draws on interviews with local residents and activists collected in the course of producing a video documentary on the disturbances of 1979. *Remembering Southall April 23rd 1979* was produced by Ross Dalziel and Shivdeep Singh Grewal in 1998 for Chok Deh Media.
2. A typical example of this was the comprehensive and compelling, yet desultory, account given by Peter Alexander, a long time Southall resident of Afro-Caribbean descent, which seamlessly merged into a single day the community resistance of 1979 with that of 1981.
3. Walter Benjamin, 'Theses on the Philosophy of History', *Illuminations* (London, 1992).
4. ibid.
5. ibid., p.254.
6. *Southall, 23 April 1979: The Report of the Unofficial Committee of Enquiry*, Published for the Committee by the National Council for Civil Liberties (NCCL), p.21.
7. Several local activists interviewed in the course of this research suggested that the arrival of Mr Ali and Socialist Unity, a group with little previous association with Southall, was regarded as a somewhat opportunist electoral strategy, and one, moreover, indicative of indifference to local organisations such as the IWA and the SYM. As noted later in the essay, this was not untypical of the attitude of local organisations toward groups on the radical left which were often perceived to be working in Southall for the good of their own organisations.
8. *Southall: The Birth of a Black Community* (The Institute of Race Relations and Southall Rights, 1981), pp.43–4.
9. *Southall, 23 April 1979*, p.7.
10. ibid., p.7.
11. ibid., p.45.
12. ibid., p.49.
13. ibid., p.38.
14. *Southall: The Birth of a Black Community*, p.3.
15. Arthur Marwick, *British Society Since 1945* (Harmondsworth, 1990), p.221.
16. *Southall, 23 April 1979*, p.77.
17. ibid., pp.77–82.
18. ibid., p.55.
19. *Southall Gazette*, 18 May 1979.
20. *Southall, 23 April 1979*, pp.54–64.
21. This was the number quoted by the home secretary. The Southall Defence Committee referred to a figure of 342.
22. *Southall, 23 April 1979*, pp. 10–12, 108–9. *Southall: The Birth of a Black Community*, pp.60–1, 35–6.

23. *Southall, 23 April 1979*, p.71.
24. Jürgen Habermas, *The Structural Transformation of the Public Sphere* (London, 1989).
25. Noam Chomsky and Edward S. Herman, *Manufacturing Consent* (New York, 1994), pp. 3–4.
26. ibid., p.3.
27. Paul Gilroy, 'Urban Social Movements, "race" and community', in Williams and Chrisman (eds), *Colonial Discourse and Post-Colonial Theory: A Reader* (Harvester Wheatsheaf, 1994).
28. John DeWitt, *Indian Workers' Associations in Britain* (Oxford, 1969), p.4.
29. ibid., p.19.
30. ibid., p.6–15.
31. *Southall: The Birth of a Black Community*, p.7.
32. DeWitt, *Indian Workers' Associations*, p.54–5.
33. ibid., p.45–7.
34. Southall: *The Birth of a Black Community*, p.10–11.
35. Dennis Morris, *Southall—A Home From Home: A Photographic Journey Through Little India* (Olympus Cameras, 1999), p.44.
36. *Southall: The Birth of a Black Community*, p.8.
37. ibid., p.25.
38. The SRA was affiliated to the nationwide Racial Preservation Societies (RPS) that arose across Britain in the early 1960s; see ibid., p.40.
39. ibid., pp.25–6.
40. Keen to counteract this image of themselves as inherently unclean and disorderly and to compensate for the progressive neglect of refuse services by the local council, the Asian residents of Southall initiated a 'Tidy the Town' initiative in 1966. This project was successfully imitated by an Asian resident who started the Southall Environment Group in 1978. He was later elected as a councillor on the strength of his 'Clean Up Southall' events. See *Southall: The Birth of a Black Community*, pp.29–30.
41. Arjun Appadurai, 'Disjuncture and difference in the global cultural economy', in Williams and Chrisman (eds), *Colonial Discourse*, p.328.
42. DeWitt, *Indian Workers' Associations in Britain*, p.60.
43. *Morning Star*, 7 June 1976.
44. DeWitt, *Indian Workers' Associations*, pp.70–2.
45. Kalra, Hutnyk and Sharma, 'Re-sounding (anti)racism, or concordant politics? Revolutionary antecedents', in Sharma, Hutnyk and Sharma (eds), *Dis-Orienting Rhythms: The Politics of the New Asian Dance Music* (London, 1996), p.130. Such factionalism did not necessarily reflect as deep a level of ideological commitment as Kalra, Hutnyk and Sharma suggest, particularly if DeWitt's accounts of the extent to which many IWA CPers were in fact apolitical opportunists is taken into account.
46. DeWitt, *Indian Workers' Associations*, p.3.
47. ibid., p.67.
48. Appadurai, 'Disjuncture and difference', p.329.

49. DeWitt, *Indian Workers' Associations*, pp.66–71. One Asian member of the CPGB remarked 'We say in India it is easier to get into the IAS (India's elite service corps) than into the Communist Party...You can join the Communist Party in this country just by filling out a blank in the *Morning Star*' (p.66).
50. A term originally coined to encompass anti-industrial/bureaucratic/nuclear, women's, youth, peace, ecology and ethnic minority movements, Gilroy concerns himself most strongly with the latter groups in the UK. In light of such a focus, the territorial dimension mentioned earlier in this article is of particular salience. Paul Gilroy, 'Urban social movements', p.405.
51. ibid., p.410.
52. *Southall: The Birth of a Black Community*, p.12.
53. Jürgen Habermas, *The Theory of Communicative Action: The Critique of Functionalist Reason* (Cambridge, 1987).
54. DeWitt, *Indian Workers' Associations*, p.48.
55. ibid., p.136.
56. Randall Hansen, *Citizenship and Immigration in Post-War Britain* (Oxford, 2000).
57. Henry Pelling, *A History of British Trade Unionism* (Harmondsworth, 1987), pp.259–60.
58. Southall: *The Birth of a Black Community*, pp.13–4.
59. DeWitt, *Indian Workers' Associations*, p.139.
60. ibid., p.144. Accounts differ between DeWitt and the writers of *Southall: The Birth of a Black Community* on the extent to which the IWA contributed to the organisation of the Woolf's strike, with DeWitt very sceptical of claims by the IWA that it was the main recruiter and mobiliser.
61. ibid., pp.140–1.
62. *Southall: The Birth of a Black Community*, pp.14–15.
63. *Between Two Cultures: A Study of Relationships between Generations in the Asian Community in Britain* (Community Relations Commission, 1976).
64. ibid.
65. BBC Radio Interview, 24 April 1979.
66. *Between Two Cultures*.
67. Gita Sahgal, 'Fundamentalism and the multi-culturalist fallacy', in *Against the Grain: Southall Black Sisters 1979–1989* (Southall Black Sisters, 1990).
68. J.P.S. Uberoi, 'Martyrdom', A paper presented at *The Sikh Spirit: A Symposium on the Issues Facing the Khalsa at 300*, New Delhi, April, 1999, p.52.
69. *Southall, 23 April 1979*, p.71.
70. Uberoi, 'Martyrdom', p.53.
71. ibid., p.53.
72. Interview with Balraj Puriwal 14 February 1999.
73. In the 1970s, 'black' was commonly adopted as the umbrella term for all ethnic minority communities, both in Southall and elsewhere: see *Against the Grain*, p.10.
74. Sahgal, 'Fundamentalism', pp.22–3.
75. ibid., pp.44–5. Sahgal illustrates the fragile balance involved in retaining an

awareness of police racism while attempting to address instances of violence by black men against women.
76. Paul Gilroy, 'Urban social movements' , p.410.
77. ibid.
78. Homi Bhabha, 'Remembering Fanon: self, psyche and the colonial condition' in Williams and Chrisman, *Colonial Discourse*, p.112.
79. *Morning Star*, 26 May 1976.
80. *Southall: The Birth of a Black Community*, p.40.
81. ibid., p.41.
82. Richard Thurlow, *Fascism in Britain: A History, 1918–1985* (Oxford, 1987), p.296.
83. Hansen, *Citizenship and Immigration*.
84. Arthur Marwick, *British Society*, p.223.
85. Pelling, *History of British Trade Unionism*, p.276.
86. ibid., p.223.
87. Kalra, Hutnyk and Sharma, 'Re-Sounding (Anti)Racism', pp.129–31.
88. Homi Bhabha, 'Remembering Fanon', p.112.
89. Kalra, Hutnyk and Sharma, 'Re-Sounding (Anti)Racism'.
90. Interview with Balraj Puriwal.
91. Jürgen Habermas, *The New Conservatism* (Polity Press, 1994), p.25.
92. William Keegan, *The Spectre of Capitalism: The Future of the World Economy After the Fall of Communism* (Vintage, 1993), p.57.
93. ibid., p.57.
94. ibid., p.57.
95. ibid., p.61.
96. Nancy Murray, 'Anti-racists and other demons: the press and ideology in Thatcher's Britain', *Racism and the Press in Thatcher's Britain* (Institute of Race Relations, 1989), pp.1–7.
97. ibid., pp.1–6.
98. DeWitt, *Indian Workers' Associations*, pp.34–5.
99. Marwick, *British Society*, p.216.
100. Hansen, *Citizenship and Immigration*.
101. Paul Foot, *Immigration and Race in British Politics* (Harmondsworth, 1965), p.44.
102. Hansen, *Citizenship and Immigration*, p.26.
103. Interview with Suresh Grover 14 February 1999.
104. *Policing Against Black People*, (Institute of Race Relations, 1987), p.viii.
105. Paul Gilroy, 'Managing the "underclass": a further note on the sociology of race relations in Britain', *Race and Class*, vol. 22, no.1, summer 1980, p.48.
106. Martin Kettle, 'The Drift to Law and Order' in Stuart Hall and Martin Jacques (eds), *The Politics of Thatcherism*, (London, 1987), pp.226–31.
107. Marwick, *British Society*, p.213.
108. ibid., p.271.
109. *Daily Telegraph*, 25 April 1979, p.2.
110. *Southall, 23rd April 1979*, pp.98–100.
111. Thurlow, *Fascism in Britain*, p. 251.

112. This term is used by Giner and Sevilla to distinguish democratic corporatism from its fascist, though still corporatist, cousin. S. Giner and E. Sevilla, 'Spain: From Corporatism to Corporatism' in A. Williams (ed.), *Southern Europe Transformed: Political and Economic Changes in Greece, Italy, Portugal and Spain* (1984).
113. Thurlow, *Fascism in Britain*, pp.26–36.
114. ibid., pp.16–8.
115. ibid., pp.245–6.
116. ibid., 70–7 and 252–7. Jordan had actually been in disgrace for some time due to his prosecution for stealing ladies underwear, ibid., p.282. His return to politics with the BM was short lived as younger enthusiasts soon took over the movement.
117. ibid., p.104.
118. ibid., p.263.
119. ibid., p.277.
120. ibid., p.xvii.
121. ibid., p.290.
122. Cross membership between the NF and the Conservative Party, such as that sought by Councillor R. Tonge, Mayor of Stafford, was increasingly common at the time, *Morning Star*, 1 June 1976.
123. Thurlow, *Fascism in Britain*, p.290.
124. ibid., pp.282–4.
125. ibid.
126. Walter Benjamin, 'Theses on the Philosophy of History', *Illuminations* (London, 1992 edn), p.249.

Ireland and British Politics

Keith Copley

Any understanding of the significance of Ireland and the Irish in British politics must take shape against the background of the colonial relationship that existed between the two countries. Britain's colonial empire was already a substantial concern by the 1830s, consisting of India, the Caribbean, Canada, South Africa and Australia, making it the largest imperial power in the world. The British ruling class had for long seen control over Ireland as of the utmost strategic importance. It enabled them to exploit the country's agricultural wealth, and it prevented Ireland becoming a base for any rival foreign power, previously Spain but later most notably France. Once the Protestant Ascendancy had proved unreliable in serving British interests, the Act of Union was passed at the turn of the century, achieved through a combination of bribery, the carrot of religious emancipation for the Catholic middle class, and the chief weapon of colonial rule—repression. As many as 137,000 troops were poured into Ireland to prevent any public protest against the plan.

Ireland's economy had been moulded to serve British interests. By the close of the seventeenth century English woollen manufacturers felt their cheaper Irish rivals were threatening their trade. Their pressure led to the English parliament passing an act prohibiting the export of raw wool to anywhere other than England. The policy was highly successful, so much so that by 1838 the once impressive Irish woollen industry was supplying only 14 per cent of its own domestic market.[1] This was not the first time direct legislation had been passed to suppress any challenge to Britain's economic power. The Cattle Act of 1666 had decimated the Irish livestock trade, which had been causing a fall in agricultural prices and, in 1696, the Navigation Acts had prohibited Ireland from direct trade with the colonies. In 1735 and again in 1746, orders were passed prohibiting the export of Irish glass.

Despite this, by the time of the Industrial Revolution, Ireland had made some steps towards industrialisation. The Act of Union of 1801, by any reckoning, had a disastrous effect on such early domestic manufacturing. At the turn of the century there had been 56 blanket manufacturers in Kilkenny, employing around 3,000 workers. By 1822, this number had been reduced to 925. There had been 2,500 calico looms at work at Balbriggan, which by 1841 had become 226. In Dublin, there had been over 4,000 employed in the woollen trade and 2,500 silk weavers, reduced by 1840 to 602 and 250 respectively.[2] In 1847, the Irish nationalist Thomas Meagher remarked bitterly that: 'One business alone survives!…That fortunate business—which the Union Act has not struck down—that favoured, and privileged, and patronised business is the Irish coffin-maker's.'[3]

Absentee landlords

The punitive results of the Act of Union was really only a continuation and intensification of traditional British policy towards Ireland. No branch of Irish industry, be it cotton, glass, brewing or shipping, escaped a colonial strategy geared towards 'restricting Irish production to the supply of raw materials for England, and crushing every manufacture which came into competition with British industry'.[4] Such distortion of the local economy was to become a feature of colonial expansion elsewhere in the world. The result for Ireland was to be, as John Saville describes, the 'decline of handicraft, the elimination of alternative employment to agriculture and the consequent loss of family income', which could only reinforce the 'growing problems in the rural areas'.[5] It certainly meant that the landlord class could 'dictate its own terms', the result of which was 'Enormous rents, low wages, farms of an enormous extent, let by rapacious and indolent proprietors to *monopolising landjobbers*, to be relet by intermediate oppressors, for five times their value, among the wretched starvers on potatoes and water'.[6] The Irish Poor Law Commission estimated in the 1830s that £10,000,000 a year went to absentee landlords, whilst an even greater sum went to middlemen and moneylenders. Only a small fraction of Ireland's agricultural wealth went to the peasantry.[7]

Many middle-class commentators were highly critical of these landlords, whom they viewed as parasitic and unproductive. The civil servant Sir Charles Trevelyan, effectively in control of government policy with regard to the Irish Famine from 1847, set out an alternative in the form of the growth of an agrarian entrepreneurial class, 'men who will carry on agriculture as a business'.[8] In one form or another, this was essentially the remedy proposed by all liberal commentators. Conditions had to be created for the 'natural' regulation of the free market to operate. Although absentee landlordism was often cited as a barrier to this, most liberal economic thought could not countenance direct government interference in relations between landlord and tenant. For, despite Ireland being the 'bulwark of the English landed aristocracy', the liberal middle class shared a common interest, as Marx put it, 'in turning Ireland into mere pasture land which provides the English market with meat and wool at the cheapest possible prices', which along with evictions and forced emigration, allowed English capital to 'function there with security'.[9]

The vast majority of middle-class discussion around Ireland took for granted, therefore, a colonialist view of a subject people who, due to their lack of English characteristics, or specifically those associated with a confident English middle class, could not lift themselves out of a poverty of their own making. *The Times* spelt this out in 1843, when it concluded that 'Ireland and the Irish have, in a great measure themselves to thank for their poverty and want of capital...It is by industry, toil, perseverance, economy, prudence, by self-denial, and self-dependency, that a State becomes mighty and its people happy'.[10] When Poor Law Commissioners visited Ireland, they would invariably agree that the poor were chiefly responsible for their own poverty. One commissioner reported that, 'if you point out the circumstances to the peasantry themselves, and endeavour to reason with them and show them how easily they might improve their condition and increase their comfort, you are invariably met with excuses as to their poverty'. On entering one peasant cottage, where women and children were found seated on the floor 'surrounded by pigs and poultry', he ascribes this condition to 'indolence', whilst the wife is 'too slatternly to sweep the floor', the man is to be found 'idly basking in the sun' and, the commissioner is careful to note, has 'not denied himself the enjoyment of whisky'.[11]

Nassau Senior was a Whig economic advisor and professor of political economy at Oxford who wrote extensively on Ireland, often contributing his thoughts to the pages of the Whig *Edinburgh Review*. Whilst he vehemently opposed increased rights for Irish tenants, and believed it 'absurd' to complain that rents were excessive, he too located the source of the problem in the absence of a sufficiently enterprising middle class, which had retarded 'the diffusion of moral and intellectual cultivation necessary for economic progress'.[12] As colonialism itself could not be held to blame, Senior concluded that there were two principal evils afflicting Ireland, one 'material' and the other 'moral.' At times it appears that he believes the material evils, 'the want of capital, and the want of small proprietors', had produced the moral ones: 'Insecurity, Ignorance, and Indolence'. However, after a discussion in which he weighs up the 'three choices' facing Ireland—the home-grown generation of capital, the introduction of capital from abroad, or the seemingly ever-present prospect of social revolution—Senior decides that only the English and Scottish middle class can rescue Ireland, but then is forced to address the question of why this had not happened and in doing so arrives back at the moral defects of the Irish to provide him with an explanation. 'It is obvious,' he muses, 'that there is something in the institutions of Ireland, or in the habits of her people, which deters British capital from one of its most natural, and apparently one of its most productive employments. It is obvious, in short, that it must be the moral evils of Ireland which exclude the remedies for her material needs.'[13] This idea of a morally defective Celtic character enjoyed wide currency amongst the middle class. In 1847, *Fraser's Magazine* compared the character traits of the English and Irish:

> The English people are naturally industrious—they prefer a life of honest labour to one of idleness. They are a persevering as well as energetic race, who for the most part comprehend their own interests perfectly, and seduously pursue them. Now of all the Celtic tribes, famous everywhere for their indolence and fickleness as the Celts everywhere are, the Irish are admitted to be the most idle and more fickle. They will not work if they can exist without it. Even here in London…the Irish labourers are the least satisfactory to deal with.[14]

It naturally followed that no amount of effort on the part of government would have any drastic effect on the conditions of such a lost cause as the Irish people. This was a particularly reassuring argument to fall back on when the sheer level of Irish immiseration led to calls from some quarters for more positive government intervention. As mounting numbers of Irish immigrants arrived in Liverpool to escape the effects of the Great Famine, the *Liverpool Mercury* launched the following attack:

> It is not to be forgotten that much, very much of Irish misery lies quite beyond the reach of any 'remedial measures' of government, being seated in the character of the Irish people…We may see of what stuff the 'finest peasantry in the world' are made of by visiting the Irish quarter in any of the large towns of England or America. There is a taint of inferiority in the character of the pure Celt which has more to do with his present degradation than Saxon domination.[15]

The onset of the Great Famine in 1845 had naturally placed all remedies for Ireland into sharp focus. When the Whig administration took over in 1846, three principal figures were to shape policy with regard to Ireland and the Famine. They were the chancellor of the exchequer Charles Wood, the colonial secretary Earl Grey, and, as already mentioned, Sir Charles Trevelyan, who did most to provide an intellectual justification for a policy which increasingly blended an evangelical Christian providentialism with a peculiarly callous liberal economic outlook, which viewed the catastrophe as the 'appointed time of Ireland's regeneration'.[16] The main efforts of Lord John Russell's government were geared towards reducing the direct costs of what relief measures existed, achieved by transferring the cost of such schemes to local Poor Law taxation. This led to a situation where, in 1848 and 1849, only £156,000 and £114,000 respectively was contributed directly by central government to relief operations. After 1847, entitlement to what relief measures existed also depended upon a whole series of means-tested conditions. The infamous 'Gregory Clause', named after the Dublin MP William Gregory, stipulated that anyone owning more than a quarter acre of land was disqualified from receiving assistance either inside or outside the workhouse, a truly barbaric measure which could only serve to intensify the already unprecedented level of misery and destitution which existed in the country. Not satisfied with this, in May 1849 the government attempted to introduce a new tax of 6d. in the pound, known as the Rate-In-Aid tax.

This is not to suggest that the previous Tory administration of Robert Peel had been much more generous. In fact, during the whole famine period the British government provided just over £10,000,000, most of it in the form of loans.[17] Whatever differences in detail that may have existed amongst policy-makers in the Whig camp, virtually all shared 'the low priority...placed on the preservation of human life—and a wilful blindness towards the agonies of the Irish population in the midst of famine'.[18] Benjamin Jowett, master of Balliol College, Oxford, was apparently referring to Senior when he remarked, 'I have always felt a certain horror of political economists since I heard one of them say that he feared the Famine of 1848 in Ireland would not kill more than a million people, and that would scarcely be enough to do much good'.[19]

An overlap of contempt

Divisions did emerge between 'optimists' and 'pessimists' when it came to the improvability of the Irish national character. The middle-class radical economist and MP George Poulett Scrope represented, along with John Stuart Mill and others, possibly the most optimistic variant of opinion amongst his class with regard to such matters, writing that 'The Irishman is neither idle, disorderly, nor savage by nature. Give him a motive for industry, and the opportunity for exerting it, and neither Englishman nor Scotchman will surpass him in close and patient toil, frugality and providence'.[20] Scrope did reject the extremes of *laissez-faire*, and urged more government intervention, not only to cultivate the four million or so acres of waste land in Ireland, but also to compel landowners, under terms of generous compensation of course, to part with some of their land to be used for the purpose of 'general public utility'. Senior was amongst those who savagely condemned this policy, along with Scrope's suggestion of extending a more charitable relief to the able-bodied poor.[21]

Scrope and Mill may have ventured the farthest, both in rejecting Malthusian doctrines and in their criticism of predatory aristocratic landlords, but they too were at pains to deny any organic link between the predicament of the Irish peasantry and the colonial relationship with Britain. The chief grievance of the peasantry, Scrope argued, was the lack of any legal security 'for their maintenance by honest industry', rather than any specific *political* opposition to the Act of Union. Indeed, despite his guarded sympathy for the semi-insurgent peasant combinations that existed throughout the Irish countryside, Scrope maintained that his remedies for Ireland were designed to 'extinguish agitation, silence the outcry for Repeal, and consolidate the Union'.[22] After all, much of his writing on Ireland was aimed towards 'advising' the new administration of Lord Melbourne in 1834, and he too recommended creating a class of bourgeois farmers, a 'class of yeomanry, a class so much wanted in Ireland', although he believed government intervention was necessary to achieve this.[23]

When considering English attitudes towards a 'subordinate' group such as the Irish in the nineteenth century, it is useful is to consider what such attitudes reveal about a wider consciousness at work amongst social classes and political factions within that society. Many of the cruder examples of prejudice against the Irish during this period have been well documented, and many historians have placed such views in the context of the emergence of a systematic theory of racial hierarchy, developed and popularised to justify a global colonial empire.[24] L.P. Curtis Jnr has been prominent amongst them, asserting that by the mid-nineteenth century 'the idea of race as *the* determinant of human history and human behaviour held an unassailable position in the minds of most Anglo-Saxons'.[25] It is the case that in 1850, Robert Knox MD had published his treatise *The Races of Men: A Philosophical Enquiry into the Influence of Race Over the Destinies of Nations*, in which he had warned his readers that 'the source of all evil lies in *the race*, the Celtic race of Ireland',[26] and in the writings of Thomas Carlyle we can find the most virulent contemporary expressions of such racism. Carlyle also supported slavery, hated democracy in any form and, after visiting Ireland, described it as a 'black howling Babel of superstitious savages'.[27] Anyone who has surveyed the 'satirical' journal *Punch* from the nineteenth century will be familiar with its regular images of the ape-like savage Irishman, 'a creature manifestly between a gorilla and a Negro', as it described Irish labourers in 1862, which 'talks a sort of gibberish'.[28] Others have suggested that 'race' was in fact a minor element within a much wider hostility to what was perceived as an Irish antipathy towards British political institutions and cultural traditions.[29]

There seems no doubt that racism was a growing element in much anti-Irish propaganda from the mid-nineteenth century onwards. But it is also important to note the degree to which attitudes to the 'subject' Irish masses and the 'subject' English workers on the part of the British ruling class coalesced around this time, producing a remarkable overlap of contempt for both. For a rising middle class, whose economic and political importance had been acknowledged by the Reform Act of 1832 and the changes in local government which had accompanied it, the assumption of intellectual and moral superiority and the prescription of harsh *laissez-faire* economic dogma were not reserved for the Irish alone. Senior had made as much clear when he wrote that 'the labouring poor of every country is condemned by *nature* to a life, which is one of struggle against want...Hunger and cold are the punishments by which she represses improvidence and sloth. If we remove these punishments, we must substitute other means of repression.'.[30] In placing the working population outside the pale of the 'political nation', a specific link was drawn between the supposed characteristics of the English working class and the Irish. That is, they were morally lax, child-like, prone to irrational passions and easily led. As Dorothy Thompson has written, 'even the most sympathetic members of the middle class only empathised with a small selected part of the working class. For the mass they reserved an attitude of fear, suspicion and total lack of comprehension'.[31] At the height of the Chartist agitation of 1848, *The Economist* regretted that whilst the 'most sober, estimable, and thoughtful of the operative classes' might be trusted with the vote, they were simply too few in number in the 1840s to justify its extension, particularly when so many of the Chartist leaders appeared to be Irishmen, 'and when we remember that their acknowledged parliamentary chief and "father", as he calls himself, is also an Irishman'.[32] For *The Times*, it was clear that conceding to any demand for manhood suffrage would be to subject parliament to the 'caprices of multitudes...whose power was based on numbers, and whose combination was independent of reason'.[33]

In fact, the 'operative classes' were seen as so lacking in reason and moral cultivation that they were often reduced in much Victorian imagery to the status of animals. One historian has noted that, by the close of the eighteenth century, 'it was a general conviction that the working man was a savage, unprincipled "brute".[34] Victorian novels would play up this theme. *Punch* may have regarded the Irish dialect as a 'sort of gibberish', but English workers fared little better. In the novel *Yeast*, Charles Kingsley described the conversation of agricultural workers in Devonshire as 'half-articulate, nasal, gutteral, made up almost entirely of vowels, like the speech of savages'.[35] Such imagery reinforced both the gulf that separated the classes, along with the constant fear of what the 'mob' might do given half the chance. The middle class, says Thompson, were much like the characters in a Victorian novel, who 'acted out their lives with the knowledge that the woods around them were full of threatening and dangerous creatures, creatures without individual names, who waited their chance to emerge under cover of darkness to loot, murder, rape, fire and destroy'.[36] These fears would come to the surface whenever working people appeared to be challenging the authority of the State. Thompson quotes a passage from a letter to Mrs Henry Taylor from Aubrey de Vere in the midst of Irish and Chartist unrest in April 1848, in which he warns her that, 'When once the lower orders have felt their physical power, they are like dogs that have tasted sheep's blood'.[37] *The Times*, as might always be expected, leaves us one of the clearest examples of such repugnance in its description of a Chartist rally in May 1848, when up to 60,000 workers demonstrated through the wealthy streets of the West End to protest at the transportation of Irish nationalist leader John Mitchell. 'The matter was viewed yesterday with a disgust approaching alarm,' reported the paper. 'The procession was looked for as one looks for a serpent, toothless perhaps, but long, slimy, insidious, and unaccountable.'[38]

The terminology of disease and infection also combined with depictions of animal savagery to describe working people, and particularly their efforts to organise together. Here again, a specific link with Ireland was drawn. Irish sedition, thought *The Times*, 'invades our social system and infects its healthy constitution'.[39] James Phillip Kay, an assistant Poor Law Commissioner under the Whig government in the late 1830s, had already employed such metaphors in the work for which he is best remembered, his 1832 pamphlet *The Moral and Physical Condition of the Working Classes*. In examining the living conditions within the working-class districts of Manchester, Kay repeatedly turns to the metaphor of disease, specifically cholera, in order to articulate the concerns of the middle class. These included factory reform, poor relief, trade union organisation, opposition to the Corn Laws and so on, but underpinning it all was the immorality of the labouring population. Kay believed that the Irish acted as a 'contagious' influence on English workers. Once the disease had passed on, however, the difference between the original carrier and its victim disappears. In a recent study of Kay, Mary Poovey notes that what is striking is the way his 'discursive treatments of the Irish simply evolve, without transition, into descriptions of English workers'.[40] Such views justified the political exclusion of both groups: '...only if English workers are in some ways *like* the Irish workers is it clear why the former...should be denied political representation...English workers are more like Irish workers than they are like their English betters, who are immune from the "contagious example" the Irish present'.[41] Even Scrope shared such fears, believing that extensive Irish emigration to Britain would spread the 'gangrene of Irish poverty, Irish disaffection, and the deadly paralysis of industry and necessarily attends upon these elements of evil'.[42]

If the economic and political ties that bound the British ruling class to Ireland made it somewhat unique amongst subject colonial nations, it also meant that the Irish themselves were an integral part of British working-class experience, and one that helped to shape significantly different perceptions of the Irish amongst large numbers of working people. The connections between Irish nationalism and English radicalism pre-date the Chartist period that marks its peak. E.P. Thompson writes that ever since the activities of the United Irishmen in the late eighteenth century, 'a conscious political alliance had been maintained', although it was an alliance which proved to be 'never free from tensions'.[43] Ever since that time, the Irish have figured prominently amongst both the leading personnel and the rank-and-file of British working-class radical politics. It was in 1828 that Irish radicals in London who were critical of O'Connell formed the Association for Civil and Political Liberty, from which a line of descent can be drawn to the Chartist movement of the late 1830s and 1840s, taking in the National Union of the Working Classes in 1831 and the London Working Men's Association in 1836 along the way. The Irish trade union organiser and radical activist John Doherty has already been mentioned. Many others can join his name, particularly with the rise of Chartism. James Leach was a factory worker and an associate of Frederick Engels who settled in Manchester in 1833, and was later to be elected president of the National Charter Association. Christopher Doyle was born in Wexford, but also found his way to Manchester where he initially worked as a power loom weaver, and was active throughout the Chartist period. In 1839, he had been arrested following the abortive uprising in Newport and sentenced to nine months imprisonment. In Barnsley, a local priest called Father Patrick Ryan was a friend of the Dublin Chartist leader Patrick O'Higgins and a member of the Irish Universal Suffrage Association. Irishmen Timothy Higgins and John W. Smith were both Chartist leaders in Ashton. George White in Bradford, Henry Cronin in Northumberland, and the Irish handloom-weaver John

Lenegan in Wigan, can be added to the list. It is inconceivable that such a prominent Irish presence in the local leadership of the movement, not to mention the most prominent Chartist of all, Feargus O'Connor, did not reflect a wider Irish participation at the grassroots. In fact, in 1848 the Commander of the North reckoned half the Bradford Chartists to be Irish.[44]

The impact of emigration

Ireland was the first modern nation to experience large-scale emigration, a fact that reflected its peculiar colonial status and the horrendous levels of poverty there. 300,000 had already departed for America by 1815, although the poorer Irish tended to head for England or Scotland. The 1841 census registered 417,000 Irish-born residents in Britain. Within ten years this figure had grown to 727,000. Nevertheless, it must be borne in mind that even at its height in 1861, the numbers of the Irish-born in Britain still only represented around 3 per cent in England and 6.6 per cent in Scotland. Outside of London, the area with the highest proportion of Irish-born was Liverpool, with 17.3 per cent of the city's population in 1841, Glasgow with 16 per cent, and Manchester with 11 per cent.[45]

The *1836 Report on the State of the Irish Poor in Great Britain* was one of the most important of a huge number of parliamentary inquiries into the problems of Ireland and the impact of Irish emigration in Britain carried out during the first half of the nineteenth century. Heavily influenced by contemporary prejudice and mainly reliant on 'hostile' witnesses, it concluded that 'Irish emigration into Britain is an example of a less civilised population spreading themselves, as a kind of substratum, beneath a more civilised community; and, without excelling in any branch of industry, obtaining possession of all the lowest departments of manual labour'.[46] However, not all Irish immigrants were peasants unskilled in urban occupations. Silk and cotton workers, reacting to the erosion of Irish industry, were amongst the first to arrive in Britain and, in Lancashire in 1851, 22 per cent of the Irish-born were classified as skilled workers, comparing well to the 26 per cent of non-Irish.[47] Nevertheless it is true that the highest percentage of male Irish-born in Lancashire at this time appear in the statistics as 'labourers', many working in the docks, in transport, or in the cotton industry where they tended to be found in the lower paid areas of production such as carding and weaving. Irish women worked overwhelmingly in domestic service, although in some areas, for instance Liverpool, up to 40 per cent of Irish women had no employment outside the home at all.

The main basis of friction between English and Irish workers was the perception that the presence of large numbers of Irish labourers depressed the wages of their English counterparts. Whether this was more a perception than a reality has been disputed by historians. We know that the most intense period of growth of an Irish presence in the cotton industry also witnessed an economic boom and some *improvement* in wages.[48] But, if there were material pressures that could lead to antipathy existing between English and Irish workers, there were many factors that could encourage a common identification. Firstly, whatever the pressures involved in such an arrangement, the fact is that both groups of workers lived and worked side by side. Despite talk of Irish ghettoisation, much recent research has revealed that, even in the most concentrated areas of Irish settlement, the Irish were never totally cut off from the native population of the same class, and may not have formed such a separate sub-stratum as is sometimes supposed. In an overall survey of research into patterns of Irish settlement in Britain, Roger Swift has concluded that if there was a divide it was based on class and not ethnicity. 'In short,' he says, 'the poor Irish lived amongst the English poor, and the upwardly mobile among the English upper working or middle class.'[49]

Another frequent accusation is that the Irish were regularly used as strike-breakers. Whilst there were occasions when Irish labour was used to undermine trade union organisation, most notably in 1844 when Lord Londonderry attempted to break a strike of Durham miners by importing labour from his Irish estates, periods of intense struggle would invariably involve English and Irish workers fighting side by side, particularly as the Irish became more established in the workforce. In a dispute in Preston in 1853, the majority of Irish operatives sided with their fellow union members, and blackleg labour imported from Ireland had to face the anger of both. As we have already seen, many early Irish immigrants had brought previous trade union experience with them to Britain. Large numbers of Irish workers had taken part in the Chartist general strike of 1842, and figured prominently in many other key labour struggles around this time, as Neville Kirk has pointed out:

> As members of the shoemaking and tailoring unions in Manchester, the Irish played a part in virtually every trial of strength with employers in the 1830s and 1840s. Irishmen were amongst those who attempted to form a national weavers' organisation in 1841, and in Manchester Irish building trades labourers were solidly organised. Noted by many employers for their 'rebellious and insubordinate' character, the Irish...were as likely to be strikers as strike-breakers.[50]

Politically, the most common cause of identification between the English and Irish working class was their shared exclusion from the franchise and the widely held belief that any attempt to challenge the status quo in either country would provoke a uniformly repressive response from the Government. When the reformed parliament in 1833 attempted to pass a new Irish Coercion Act, which was to surpass all such previous Acts in the powers it conferred on the Lord Lieutenant to suppress the very sort of non-violent democratic activities English radicals regularly took part in, it presented a defining moment in the fracture of English radicalism along hostile class lines. As Dorothy Thompson writes:

> The Irish Coercion Act, the emasculation of the Factory Act, the attacks on trade unions, all contributed to the disillusion felt by working-class radicals with the Reform Act and the administration which followed it. The interests of the manufacturers and shopkeepers which had seemed to many in 1832 to be allied to those of the working people, now seemed to be being advanced in every area in which they conflicted with working-class interests.[51]

Opposition to the New Poor Law, introduced by the same Whig administration, has been generally acknowledged as a key component in laying the political groundwork for the Chartist movement. But the first working-class demonstrations against the new government were to protest at this latest Coercion Act, and it was both these issues, the hated Poor Law *and* Irish coercion, that were to provide a litmus test for radicals and reveal remarkably deep and bitter divisions within British society. The *Poor Man's Guardian* protested against the naked brutality of British rule in Ireland, declaring 'these iron-hearted devils have no bowels of compassion. It was nothing to them—gorged as they are with the wealth they have not earned—that 40,000 human beings had to live on twopence halfpenny a day. To put down the people of Ireland with the sword was the thing uppermost in their minds.'[52] It was the Irish Bill that provoked the National Union of the Working Classes into adopting a more confrontational position towards the government, calling a national convention and a series of huge meetings across the country to rally opposition to the Bill. Birmingham witnessed one of the largest radical meetings in its history; and, in Manchester, 14,000 names were gathered on a petition, and John Doherty addressed a huge gathering in the city. Those who attended and spoke at these meetings emphasised not only a clearly quite different attitude towards the Irish than that found amongst the middle class, but a clear understanding that such an injury inflicted on the Irish would be an injury inflicted on themselves also. As one speaker told a NUWC meeting in London early in the year, 'the English would have their share of it bye and bye; they would be lashed with the same scorpion if they did not exert themselves to prevent this outrage being perpetrated on the people of Ireland'.[53] At a meeting held in March, the following resolution was endorsed: 'That as the people of England are now put upon their trial, if they supinely allow their Irish brethren to be given up to the military despotism proposed by the Whigs, they will give consent to the acknowledged 'unconstitutional' measure of Earl Grey and, consequently, will be *forging chains for themselves.*'[54]

Irish nationalism and Chartism

This growth of working-class radical agitation, culminating in the birth of the Chartist movement had, then, solidarity with the Irish struggle at its very heart. The agitation around the Irish Bill led many to seek a more permanent unity between the English and Irish. The London Anti-Union Association, which had been founded by Irish immigrants in February 1832, affiliated to the NUWC in September, and the Irish became more influential within the NUWC as the 'Irish question' came to command the attention of the movement. A quarterly general meeting of the NUWC in October 1832 agreed to have repeal included as an official objective of the movement. The radical Irish journalist Bronterre O'Brien wrote shortly afterwards that, 'the people of Ireland and the people of England have the same enemies and the same friends—their enemies are those who would take their labour, or fruits of it, without an equivalent—their friends are those who would save them from the spoilators'.[55] From this time onwards, and throughout the Chartist period, consistent attempts to forge such unity were made. In 1838, the year before the official birth of Chartism, the Newcastle Working Men's Association delivered an address to the trade unionists of Dublin, and, invoking the spirit of the United Irishmen, declared: 'We calculate upon your future assistance.'[56] The Chartists themselves made serious efforts to get their first petition signed both by Irish immigrants in Britain and within Ireland itself, and the preamble to the second and largest petition in 1842 contained the demand for repeal of the Union. The first Chartist National Convention in 1839 set up a special committee to rally support in Ireland. Until the late 1840s, the influence of the Irish MP Daniel O'Connell, who as the champion of Catholic Emancipation and leader of the Repeal Association held a pre-eminent place in Irish politics, was the major barrier to achieving practical unity, and O'Connellite mobs viciously attacked Chartist meetings in Ireland in 1839. When the leadership of the Chartists attempted to influence the Irish Repeal movement in 1843 by joining branches of the Repeal Association in Britain, they were more often than not expelled or refused membership, although in some areas, notably

Barnsley, the Repeal Association was controlled by Irish immigrants who both supported O'Connell and remained sympathetic to Chartism. It was a combination of circumstances coming together in 1848 that led to the first real formal unity between Irish nationalism and Chartism. O'Connell had died the year previously, with his political reputation already severely damaged. The Great Famine gripped Ireland, leading many Irish nationalists to question previously accepted dogmas of respectability and moral force. And, crucially, revolution had broken out in Paris in February, and was soon to spread with remarkably rapidity throughout Europe, igniting resurgent revolutionary enthusiasm and expectations in both Britain and Ireland. Irish nationalism, particularly in the guise of John Mitchell and his new journal called the *United Irishman*, turned increasingly to talk of physical force and a united uprising in Ireland and Britain. Even the more mainstream leadership of the middle-class Young Ireland group, now renamed the Irish Confederation following their split with O'Connell in 1847, could see the benefit of an alliance with such a formidable force as the Chartists in the heart of the colonial power itself. There is no space here to go into detail about the events of 1848, which was to prove to be Chartism's final great challenge. Suffice to say that the call for unity was taken up with great enthusiasm, particularly in the northern manufacturing districts of Yorkshire and Lancashire, leading to a situation in which some areas were placed under virtual military siege as the year progressed. In April, *The Times* reported that 'the alarm of the British government is great, and we presume is not less so because the Irish in England are fast fraternising with the masses of the English people'.[57]

This does not mean that such solidarity did not have to be fought for. Religious and ethnic animosities existed within working-class communities, although most historians will acknowledge that their tempo and intensity took on an increase in the later half of the century. The 1830s and 1840s did witness clashes, often between English and Irish 'navvies', such as the pitched battles around Chester and Birkenhead railway in October 1839, or the riots around Penrith in 1846 that actually lasted for several days. However, during this period, Chartism was able to act as a counter-weight to such sectarian feuds. Even in Liverpool, where the Tories had established a tradition of using sectarianism for electoral favour, such attempted division did not always meet with great success in the 1840s. The Liverpool Protestant Association, set up to fight around the issue of religious education, was losing much of its support by 1841, and was in any case largely a middle-class organisation. The attempt to establish an organisation with a more working-class constituency, the Liverpool Operative Protestant

Association in 1838, had met with little support; in the mid-1840s the Orange Order had superseded these organisations. However, the active support of Orangeism in Liverpool has often been overestimated, comprising perhaps no more than 30 Orange Lodges involving no more than five to six hundred supporters. As Liverpool was already home to a sizeable Ulster Protestant community, this makes it 'conceivable that the indigenous population were not involved at all'.[58] Furthermore, if the Tories did fight the 1837 election on the 'Orange card', it served to weaken their vote amongst the working class freemen, their vote amongst this group being 2,819 in that election compared to 3,977 in 1835. 'The evidence,' concludes one historian, 'points to a minimal involvement in sectarian violence by the English-born population. While the influx of the Irish in the 1840s must have created tensions, 'No Popery' politics had nothing of the force it was to acquire in Liverpool for the best part of the next one hundred years.'[59] This does provide a contrast to the post-Chartist period, when areas such as Stockport and Ashton, previously Chartist strongholds with prominent Irish Chartist leaders, saw serious anti-Catholic rioting in 1852 and 1854. In Ashton, sectarian bigots were able to build a base in the area on the corpse of Chartism. A prominent local Orangeman stood in the 1857 parliamentary election on a platform of 'No Popery' *and* support for universal manhood suffrage.

The other side of the coin was that, with Chartism no longer a force capable of challenging religious prejudice inside the working class, and its replacement with a more timid form of single-issue campaigning, Irish workers themselves were now more often to be found at the forefront of reactionary mobs stirred up by the Catholic Church. One such incident was a radical gathering in Hyde Park in 1862 to express workers' support for the Italian nationalist Garibaldi, which was attacked by Irish Catholics. Despite both a tradition of opposition to Catholicism on the part of many English radicals and the vehement opposition of the Catholic Church to any Irish involvement in a turbulent and secular movement like Chartism, an elementary class solidarity and a shared consciousness of injustice and political exclusion had at times overridden such barriers. In short, says Swift, 'ordinary Irish Catholics were often an integral part of British proletarian culture, in which English radicals actively championed the Irish cause and sought and gained Irish Catholic support'.[60]

Some commentators have made the suggestion that internationalism was confined to a relatively small metropolitan radical elite, and did not permeate down to the grassroots of the movement.[61] D.G. Paz has suggested that the 'cheap, gutter periodicals' on sale to workers at the time, which tended to contain both anti-Catholic rants and the more demeaning portrayals of

Irish men and women, are more representative of what workers actually thought about such matters than the radical press.[62] These arguments simply underestimate the thirst for radical ideas amongst the working class. Paine's *Rights of Man* had sold 50,000 copies as far back as 1791. Cobbett's *Address to the Journeymen and Labourers* had reached a circulation of 200,000 in 1826 and, by the 1830s, Hetherington's *Poor Man's Guardian* was regularly selling 16,000.[63] Around the time of the Reform Act, there were no less than eight radical newspapers in circulation in London alone. These achievements are all the more remarkable given the fact that the 'un-stamped' press regularly faced political victimisation was often under-capitalised compared with its rivals. The most important working-class radical newspaper was undoubtedly the *Northern Star*, launched just before the birth of Chartism but which was to became its official mouthpiece, which at its height was to achieve a circulation to rival the London *Times*. The point missed by Paz, is that reading a paper like the *Northern Star* was not merely a pastime or a means of escapism, but was part of an active, collective political experience. Workers would not only read or have the paper read to them, but would send their own reports to it, ensure its distribution and organise politically around it, implying a commitment to the ideas contained within it. The evidence we have would point to the fact that a commitment to Irish freedom was taken seriously by very large numbers of working people, and was bound up with their more general social and political concerns. The earliest attempts by workers in Britain to build their own political movement had internationalism, and a particular emphasis on solidarity with the Irish, at its very core, because it understood that such solidarity struck a most direct blow against their own ruling class. Whilst the British working class has often been characterised as mired in chauvinism and racism, this is a part of our history that socialists should both understand and celebrate. In April 1848, as the Chartist Convention assembled in London in preparation for a mass rally and the presentation of another petition to parliament, the following proclamation was posted around the city:

> Irishmen resident in London, on the part of the democrats in England we extend to you the warmest hand of fraternisation; your principles are ours, and ours shall be yours. Remember the aphorism, that union is strength and division is weakness; centuries of bitter experience prove to you the truth of the latter, let us now cordially endeavour to test the virtue of the former…What an awful spectacle is Ireland, after forty-seven years of the vaunted Union! Her trade ruined, her agriculture paralysed, her people scattered over the four quarters of the globe, and her green fields in twelve months just past made the dreary graveyards of 100,000 fam-

ished human beings. Irishmen…if you detest these monstrous atrocities, unite heart and soul with those who will struggle with you to exterminate the hell-engendered cause of your country's degradation.[64]

Notes

1. L.M. Cullen, *Economic History of Ireland Since 1600* (London, 1972), p.106.
2. K. Marx, 'Outline of a Report on the Irish Question', in K. Marx and F. Engels, *Ireland and the Irish Question* (Moscow, 1971 edn), p.131.
3. Quoted in ibid, p.132.
4. E. Burns, *British Imperialism in Ireland* (London, 1931), p.7.
5. J. Saville, *1848: The British state and the Chartist movement* (Cambridge, 1987), p.30.
6. Marx, 'Outline', p.132.
7. C. Bambery, *Ireland's Permanent Revolution* (London, 1990), p.22.
8. C. Trevelyan, *The Irish Crisis* (London, 1848).
9. Quoted in J. Charlton, *It Just Went Like Tinder: The mass movement and new unionism in Britain 1889* (London, 1999), p.82.
10. *The Times*, 4 August 1843.
11. *Northern Star*, 27 September 1845.
12. N. Senior, *Conversations and Essays Relating to Ireland* (London, 1868), p.25.
13. ibid., p.33.
14. *Fraser's Magazine*, vol. 27, March 1847.
15. Quoted in F. Neal, *Sectarian Violence: The Liverpool experience, 1819–1914* (Manchester, 1988), p.114.
16. Trevelyan, *Irish Crisis*, p.200.
17. C. Kinealy, 'Potatoes, providence and philanthropy: the role of private charity during the famine', in P. O'Sullivan (ed.), *The Irish World-Wide: history, heritage, identity*, vol. 6 (Leicester, 1997), p.142.
18. P. Gray, 'Nassau Senior, the Edinburgh Review and Ireland 1843–49', in T. Foley and S. Ryder (eds), *Ideology and Ireland in the Nineteenth Century* (Dublin, 1998), p.142.
19. Quoted in L. Curtis, *The Cause of Ireland* (Belfast, 1994), p.580.
20. G.P. Scrope, *How is Ireland to be Governed?* (London, 1846), p.34.
21. Senior, *Conversations*, p.163. He condemned the policy as 'confiscation'.
22. Scrope, *How is Ireland to be Governed?*, p.39.
23. ibid., p.54.
24. See, for example, L.P. Curtis Jnr, *Apes and Angels. The Irishman in Victorian caricature* (Washington, 1997) or R.F. Foster, *Paddy and Mr Punch* (London, 1993).
25. L.P. Curtis Jnr, *Anglo-Saxons and Celts: A study in anti-Irish prejudice in Victorian England* (Connecticut, 1968), p.19.
26. R. Knox, *The Races of Men: A philosophical enquiry into the influence of race over the destiny of nations* (London, 1850), p.379.
27. Quoted in L. Curtis, *Information on Ireland* (London, 1983), p.48.
28. Quoted in R. Swift, 'The historiography of the Irish in nineteenth century

28. [cont.] Britain' in O'Sullivan (ed.), *The Irish World-Wide*, vol. 2, p.69.
29. See S. Gilley, 'English attitudes towards the Irish in England 1780–1900', in Colin Holmes (ed.), *Immigrants and Minorities in British Society* (London, 1978).
30. Senior, *Conversations*, p.190.
31. D. Thompson, *The Chartists: Popular politics in the Industrial Revolution* (Aldershot, 1984), p.251.
32. *The Economist*, 29 April 1848.
33. *The Times*, 10 July 1848.
34. J.H. Plumb, quoted in Curtis, *Anglo-Saxons and Celts*, p.40.
35. Quoted in Thompson, *Chartists*, p.249.
36. ibid., p.250.
37. ibid., p.149.
38. *The Times*, 1 June 1848.
39. *The Times*, 6 May 1848.
40. M. Poovey, 'Curing the social body in 1832: James Phillip Kay and the Irish in Manchester', in *Gender and History*, vol. 5 (summer, 1993), p.206.
41. ibid., p.207.
42. G.P. Scrope, *How to Make Ireland Self-Supporting* (London, 1848), p.28.
43. E.P. Thompson, *The Making of the English Working Class* (London, 1991 edn), p.481.
44. For more detail of Irish involvement in Chartism, see D. Thompson, 'Ireland and the Irish in English Radicalism Before 1850' in J. Epstein and D. Thompson (eds), *The Chartist Experience: Studies in working class radicalism and culture, 1830–1860* (London, 1982), and E. and R. Frow, 'Biographies of Irish Chartists', in *North West Labour History Bulletin*, no. 16 (1991/92).
45. See F. Neal, *Black 47: Britain and the Famine Irish* (London, 1998), p.5.
46. Quoted in Thompson, *English Working Class*, p.476.
47. W.J. Lowe, *The Irish in Mid-Victorian Lancashire* (New York, 1989), p.87.
48. See N. Kirk, *The Growth of Working Class Reformism in Mid-Victorian England* (London, 1985), p.329.
49. R. Swift, 'The historiography of the Irish', p.65.
50. Kirk, *Growth*, p.315.
51. Thompson, *Chartists*, p.28.
52. *Poor Man's Guardian*, 16 February 1833.
53. ibid.
54. *Poor Man's Guardian*, 2 March 1833.
55. *Poor Man's Guardian*, 3 May 1834.
56. *The Northern Liberator*, 14 April 1838.
57. *The Times*, 10 April 1848.
58. K. Moore, 'This Whig and Tory ridden town: popular politics in Liverpool in the Chartist era', in J. Belchem (ed.), *Popular Politics, Riot and Labour: Essays in Liverpool History, 1790–1930* (Liverpool, 1992), p.54.
59. ibid., p.60.
60. R. Swift, 'The historiography of the Irish', p.66.

61. See H. Weisser, *The British Working Class Movement and Europe, 1815–1848* (Manchester, 1975), p.167.
62. D. G. Paz, 'Anti-Catholicism, Anti-Irish stereotyping and Anti-Celtic racism in mid-Victorian working class periodicals', *Albion*, vol. 18 (winter, 1986).
63. R. Williams, 'The press and popular culture: an historical perspective', in G. Boyce, J. Curran and P. Wingate (eds), *Newspaper History from the Seventeenth Century To the Present Day* (London, 1978), p.43.
64. Quoted in J. Saville, *1848*, p.106.

Labour's Irish Questions 1918–81

Cronain O'Kelly

Historically, governing Ireland has proved to be highly divisive for the British ruling class. The various questions posed by ruling Ireland were to divide radicals from conservatives, and defined many of the political alignments of the nineteenth century; for example, the divisions of the Tories over Catholic Emancipation (1829) and, subsequently, the Liberals over Home Rule (1886). The coalescence of the cause of Irish nationalism with that of reform of the electoral franchise and the rise of organised Labour was mirrored by the consistent support given by the Conservatives to the Union with Ireland. It is this particular conjuncture of forces that has led many critics of British policy in Ireland to cast the Conservative Party as the natural friend of Unionism and, by corollary, Labour as the ally of Irish nationalism. The faith that has been shown towards the Labour Party by those in Britain attempting to build solidarity with Irish nationalists is evinced in the orientation of the Anti Partition League (APL) and the Troops Out Movement (TOM), established in 1945 and 1973 respectively. Both of these groups looked to Labour as a means of delivering unification. Given the unique constitutional position of Ireland, however, and the explicitly confrontational form that the assertion of Irish nationalism has taken (i.e. political violence), any expression of sympathy with republicanism has posed serious political dilemmas for socialists in Britain; this was noted by Geoffrey Bell when he argued that the attitude of the Labour Party towards Ireland shaped its very understanding of socialism.[1]

Maintaining the status quo

In practice, the Labour Party leadership has consistently sought to contain demands for Irish self-determination within terms acceptable to the constitutional status quo. Therefore, the succinct reply to Bell's rhetorical question about the Labour Party's understanding of socialism would have to conclude that, in relation to Ireland, Labour was essentially conservative.

It is the intention of this study to address what prevented the Labour Party, acting at a national parliamentary level as the major representative of the British trade union movement and, therefore, as the dominant force in British socialist politics, from challenging the consensus over Britain's relationship to Ireland. To illustrate this problem more fully it will be necessary to examine the origins and character of the Labour Party, in contrast to Irish republicanism, and its attitude towards three defining issues of the conflict: first, the way in which partition came about; secondly, the character of the successor state in the six counties; and, thirdly, the revival of republican political violence after 1970. From an examination of these key areas of policy, it may be seen that the Labour Party, in orientating itself towards the institutions of the state, has consistently subordinated the aspirations of Irish nationalists to the interests of either strategic advantage, the co-operation of the Ulster Unionists, or the continuance of bi-partisanship. In all these respects, the Labour leadership has gone as far as the Conservatives to reinforce the Union. Furthermore, it was a characteristic of the national and parliamentary leadership of the Labour Party that it was able to pursue such a policy notwithstanding any extra-parliamentary opposition from its own party activists, or from the wider movement it claimed to represent.[2]

Despite the position of the Labour movement leadership, a significant minority have argued regularly for an alliance of socialists and trade unionists in Britain with republicans and nationalists in Ireland. Making a call for support to be given to Irish nationalists necessitated mounting a direct challenge to the patriotism of British workers. As late as 1975, Mike Cooley, a British trade unionist and supporter of TOM, could point to a certain paradox in the causes championed by British socialists, that they were happy to support national liberation struggles conducted against any country other than Britain:

> Our trade union movement has repeatedly supported the campaign in respect of Vietnam, it has supported the campaign in support of those fighting in Chile, Greece, Mozambique and it's about time that we begin to support the campaign against what is going on right here on our door step.

However, there is a crucial difference in the relationship between Britain and Ireland which sets it apart from the other 'anti-Imperialist' movements to which Cooley alludes:

> Any blow against British capitalist rule in Ireland is of a hundred times greater political significance than a blow of equal weight in Asia or

Africa…The reality is the working class of this country can never be free whilst it holds others in subjection. The institutions, which were built up to suppress the Irish people, the Indian people and all those in the British colonies, have been used systematically against the British people themselves.[3]

It was the relationship of the British working class to the cause of Irish national self-determination, and more particularly their acquiescence or support for continued British rule, that concerned Marx, who in writing to German comrades in 1870 noted the antipathy felt by British workers to the Irish immigrants in British cities, but noted the disastrous consequences that this held for the British workers' struggle for an improvement of their own condition:

Compared with the Irish worker, he feels himself a member of the ruling nation and for this very reason he makes himself into the tool of the aristocrats and capitalist against Ireland and thus strengthens their domination over himself…This antagonism is the secret of the impotence of the English working class, despite its organisation.[4]

For those who followed Marx in the revolutionary tradition, particularly Lenin, support for nationalism was not an end in itself; rather, the support that workers may have given to any call for national self-determination was, and is, conditional upon it being made by an 'oppressed' against an 'oppressor' nation.[5] For the working class of the oppressor country, it was believed to be vital in its own struggle for socialism that it should support the demand for self-determination of the oppressed nation.[6] Here then, was the unique nature of Irish national self-determination and its practical form in republicanism: it was a direct challenge to the hegemony of the British ruling class within its own borders. This challenge provided revolutionaries with the opportunity to encourage the British working class to take sides against its own rulers, and to support those who challenged the same state that British workers were on occasion drawn into conflict with as a result of fighting for their own class interests.

For the Labour Party, the issue of Irish national self-determination was extremely problematic, and exposed the immaturity of the political leadership of the British working class, despite the supposed common enemy of the Conservative Party (the domestic ally of Ulster Unionism). Irrespective of the reverence with which British socialists, both reformist and revolutionary, regarded Labour, it must be remembered that it emerged only belatedly from the tutelage of the Liberal Party. The Labour Representation Committee originated as the parliamentary voice for the trade union movement in Britain, consciously eschewing wider political questions. It was not until 1918 that the Labour Party reached its zenith of socialistic intent with adoption of 'clause four' into its constitution, committing Labour to the goals of the redistribution of wealth and public ownership.

Despite its political weakness, the Labour Party exerted an almost mesmeric influence upon those in and outside of its ranks; effectively choking off attempts to build a more combative form of working-class politics. The revolutionary left became increasingly isolated following the Cold War, even after its post-1960s revival, and at a national level, it deferred largely to the Labour Party as being a vehicle through which socialism could be achieved in Britain.[7] The idea of using physical force to defend the Labour movement would have seemed highly controversial, and the idea of the direct overthrow of the state apparatus would have been regarded as treasonous.

The historical experience of the British Labour movement led it to regard the security aspect of the state as being politically neutral; this attitude only began to change following the unusually violent industrial disputes of the 1970s and 1980s. It was characteristic of reformist socialist parties to look to the state to enact reforms such as the provision of welfare: the British Labour movement had been fortunate in the absence of any major direct conflict with the state, as had characterised class relations in France (1871), Italy (1898), or Germany (1919). Similarly, the Labour Party differed radically from the tradition of Irish republicanism—and indeed many socialist movements in Europe—in its attitude to the institutions of the state, which has been demonstrated in the Labour Party's historic respect for parliament.[8]

A necessary reform

It is unsurprising that so violent an opposition to British rule would have proved deeply unpalatable to the Labour Party. Given that it had emerged from the 'womb' of British Liberalism, it could be assumed that the Parliamentary Labour Party (PLP) absorbed the defence of the Union as an axiomatic principle. Certainly, constitutional historians of the nineteenth century linked patriotism in general, and the British variant in particularly, to the defence of the constitution.[9] The importance of the defence of the constitution to national political life can be demonstrated in that the Liberal Party had failed to remain unified over the limited autonomy proposed for Ireland under Home Rule by Gladstone in 1886. Whilst the Labour Party may have shared the Liberals' Whiggish veneration for the parliamentary tradition, it could be far more detached in its support for Home Rule. As Bell notes:

> The Party representatives argued, when they bothered to apply their minds to the subject, that Home Rule was no more than a necessary reform,

unexceptional in its implications, good for the Irish working class, good for Ireland and good for Britain.[10]

This apparently pragmatic view was shared by Winston Churchill, who justified this 'sentimental point' on the grounds of winning Ireland's support for the empire in time of war.[11] Whether Labour's support for Home Rule was informed by Fabian pragmatism or a similar emotional attachment to the Union that characterised the Conservatives response, the conclusions were remarkable in their similarity.[12] From the point of view of socialists in Britain, this meant that the Labour Party leadership shared the same position as the Conservatives and Ulster Unionists in the maintenance of the empire and the containment of Irish national self-determination.

Sinn Fein's election victory in 1918 and the establishment of the independent *Dail Eireann* the following year returned the issue of the Union to British politics. The 'physical force' tradition of Irish nationalism stood in stark contrast to the generally pacific nature of British politics. However, given Ireland's historical experience of invasion and enforced absorption by a larger unit, this difference is unsurprising. Irish republicanism had been the most militant expression of Irish nationalism in the twentieth century, calling for the complete national sovereignty of the thirty-two counties to be exercised by the whole of the people of the island of Ireland acting as a single entity without British interference. republicanism drew upon the iconography of previous struggles against British rule in Ireland and it was its most militant section, the Irish Republican Army (IRA), which drew its own legitimacy from its role as defender of the Dáil. For the IRA, the legitimacy of *Dail Eireann* was crucial; this was the last all-Ireland government formed before Britain imposed partition in 1921. Therefore, the IRA has regarded the subsequent governments established in the successor states of the twenty-six counties in the 'South', and the six counties in the 'North', as illegitimate regimes; any retreat from these positions by the leadership of the republican movement has resulted in schisms (1922, 1928, 1948 or 1969). The consistent position adhered to by classical republicanism was that only the IRA was the true heir to the revolutionary government established by the election of 1918, and that they alone could end partition and liberate Ireland from British rule.

Fault line in British politics

Once again, Ireland marked a fault line in British politics, this time between the Labour movement and its parliamentary representatives. The leadership of the Labour Party opposed the 'extra parliamentarianism' of the declaration of independence,[13] whereas the newspaper of the Communist Party of Great Britain (CPGB), *The Communist,* called upon the Labour Party to recognise the Irish republic as an established fact.[14] The question of national security, and security of the empire as a whole, was used by the Labour leadership to limit these demands to Home Rule within the empire in the face of popular support for Irish national self-determination. In April 1919, the Second International adopted a position of support for full and complete Irish independence; in 1920, the Labour Party conference passed a resolution in favour of complete and unconditional independence for Ireland; and, in August 1920, local 'Councils of Action' (established to prevent Britain sending guns to Poland to fight the Soviet government) began to advocate direct action in support of Ireland. By September, even the *Manchester Guardian* advocated strike action to stop the 'Tan War'.[15] In December 1920, the Labour Party had sent a commission of inquiry to Ireland and, at the end of the month, presented its findings to a special party conference on Ireland. Delegates were invited only to accept or reject the resolution; no amendments were allowed. The resolution called for the withdrawal of troops and self-determination on condition of the security of the empire and the protection of minorities. The Labour Party leadership welcomed partition as an amicable solution to the Irish question, with the leader of the PLP, J. R. Clynes, even referring to it as triumph of national patriotism.[16] The Treaty of Partition closed the 'old' Irish question whilst simultaneously posing a new one; that of Britain's relationship to the two successor states that had emerged, in particular the character of the Northern Irish state and Britain's influence over it.

The 1949 Government of Ireland Act may be seen as the next major legislative episode in Labour's relationship with Ireland; this was significant as it made an explicit statement reinforcing Northern Ireland's position within the Union conditional upon the will of the Northern Ireland parliament. The formal dynamic for this change was external; that is, the change in the relationship between the United Kingdom and the Dublin government when the latter repealed the External Relations Act. The Irish Free State was a product of the war of independence and the partition treaty imposed upon the Dail in 1921. In 1938, the Irish constitution was altered to include specific reference to partition and a claim to sovereignty over the six counties of Northern Ireland. In 1949, the Irish constitution was changed again when Eire (as the Free State was renamed after 1938) declared herself a republic and left the Commonwealth.

The response of the British government in the form of the 1949 Act was made partly at the behest of the Unionist government of Northern Ireland, but it also reflected the sympathies of the Labour cabinet, Herbert Morrison in particular, coupled with the desire to maintain the strategic advantages that bases in the six counties were presumed to hold.[17] There were no changes to the repressive aspects of the Northern Irish state; Atlee failed in persuading the Northern Irish prime minister (Basil Brook) to lower the duration of the residential qualifications for either the Westminster or Stormont franchises and, in 1951, the Labour home secretary, Chuter Ede, defended Stormont's use of the Northern Ireland Special Powers Act as necessary to combat the IRA.[18]

Labour backbenchers were active in criticising their own administration over its policy towards the Northern Ireland government, in particular its use of the Special Powers Act. However, the orientation of this criticism began to take a new form away from the traditional aim of unification of Northern Ireland with the twenty-six counties. The sources of the shift in orientation were manifold, although changes in the domestic and international political order could be seen as providing an environment in which a rethinking of Britain's relationship to Ireland seemed possible. The 1945 general election had resulted in Labour's first landslide victory; the party had come to power on a programme of universal welfare and public ownership; the *laissez-faire* model of capitalism had been discredited through the experience of the depression and war. Clearly, many Labour activists and MPs believed that real social and political change was possible; even the character of the nation and empire seemed to be undergoing metamorphosis.[19] The legacy of the struggle against fascism, and the political environment of the Cold War, provided a new focus for opposition to British policy in relation to Northern Ireland emphasising human rights.

Within the PLP, the Friends of Ireland (FI) group led the agitation on the general character of Northern Ireland. The FI group was established in 1945 by the Manchester Labour MP Hugh Delargy, and had connections with the Anti-Partition League active in Ireland and Britain (also established in 1945). The opposition that the FI offered to the Labour Party leadership essentially focused upon the failure of Northern Ireland to live up to the same standards of civil and political rights enjoyed elsewhere in Britain.[20] It should be noted that the heterogeneity of this group reflected the subtle shift in the criticism levelled at British policy in Ireland. Members such as Henry McGhee and Hugh Delargy were traditional republicans, favouring a united Ireland. By contrast, Geoffrey Bing advocated the integration of the six counties into the rest of the United Kingdom. In his 1950 pamphlet *John Bull's other Ireland,* Bing described the unique problem that Northern Ireland posed; citing Section 75 of the Government of Ireland Act 1920, he noted that the Westminster parliament retained supreme authority over Stormont; therefore, Bing argued, the actions of the Northern Ireland government were (albeit partly) the responsibility of the British electorate.[21]

Bing's pamphlet highlighted many of the abuses, such as religious discrimination and electoral malpractice, which were later lighted upon by the Campaign for Democracy in Ulster (CDU) in the Labour Party and the Northern Ireland Civil Rights Association (NICRA) nearly twenty years later.[22] However, what is particularly noteworthy is that Bing, and the later critics of Stormont, saw the source of the inequalities in Northern Ireland as lying in too much autonomy from Westminster.[23] Commenting specifically upon the Special Powers Act, Bing objected to the potential delegation of powers to an individual police officer and the consequent lack of accountability.[24] Thus, Bing's departure from previous critics of the Labour Party's policies on Ireland (and his contemporaries in the FI) was that the position he took appeared to mark the emergence on the part of the Labour left of the belief in the viability of a reformed Northern Irish state.

The belief in the possibility of the reform of Northern Ireland sustained the pressure placed upon Stormont by the Labour governments headed by Harold Wilson (1964–70) and, more immediately, by both CDU and NICRA, organisations that emphasised their desire to apply equal standards to issues such as housing and electoral representation in Northern Ireland, rather than unification with the republic. This situation was compounded by the republican movement's increased concentration upon social and economic issues following the failure of the military campaign it had waged from 1956 to 1962. By 1969, the desire to end partition on the part of nationalists within Northern Ireland appeared to have declined so acutely that the civil rights activists Bernadette Devlin and Ivan Cooper could demand the introduction of direct rule.[25] When troops were sent to Northern Ireland in August 1969, their arrival was welcomed not only by nationalists but also by many groups on the left in Britain, including the International Socialists (IS) and CPGB.[26]

The election of a Conservative government in June 1970 has been suggested as a reason for the deterioration of relations between the republicans and the British army;[27] however, this should be balanced against the strong bi-partisan approach to the issue of Ireland that existed between the Labour and Conservative Parties. Indeed, the record of Labour home and Northern Ireland secretaries demonstrates an approach of antipathy towards unruly republicans equal to that of the Conservatives. The record of James Callaghan as Labour home secretary is illustrative of this approach; when in office he supported the use of lethal force against nationalist rioters.[28]

When in opposition, Callaghan continued in his co-operation with the Conservative government. Even following the introduction of internment and 'Bloody Sunday', Labour criticised the Heath administration not on principle but on an assessment of its effectiveness in containing the 'National Question'.[29] The military campaign mounted by republicans had underlined the volatility of Northern Ireland and its difference from the rest of the United Kingdom.[30]

Drive for 'normalisation'

In marked contrast to the Heath administration, Labour attempted to contain, and ultimately defeat, republican political violence by refusing to address it as a political question at all. After their return to government, the content of Labour policy towards the IRA redefined the war as being one against a criminal rather than political opponent; Labour Northern Ireland secretaries Merlyn Rees and his successor Roy Mason asserted repeatedly Northern Ireland's 'British-ness' and the feasibility of military victory over the IRA, evinced by Rees' response to the IRA ceasefire of 1975.[31] Mason's dual emphasis upon economics and security can be seen as part of a drive to 'normalise' the situation in Northern Ireland and to strengthen the provinces' relationship to the rest of the United Kingdom. Mason made frequent reference to the successful use of the security forces in defeating the IRA, granted Northern Ireland greater representation at Westminster with the creation of six additional constituencies (raising the total number of seats for Northern Ireland from twelve to eighteen), and increased the level of public sector spending relative to the rest of the United Kingdom.[32]

In terms of legal restraints upon suspected members of paramilitary groups, the incoming Labour government inherited the no jury 'Diplock' Courts (introduced under the Northern Ireland Emergency Provisions Act 1973) and increased them with the introduction of the Prevention of Terrorism Act (PTA), itself a response to the Birmingham and Guildford pub bombings. Much of Labour's drive for 'normalisation' derived from the Gardiner Inquiry, held in January 1975, which pointed to the granting of special category status to those convicted of terrorist offences as being a mistake; it had, by implication, conferred legitimacy upon the activities of the respective paramilitaries. Gardiner recommended a policy of criminalisation, which meant the withdrawal of this special category status and in effect a denial of political legitimacy to paramilitary prisoners; this was implemented in 1976.

These shifts in security policy towards criminalisation did not have the desired results for the Labour government, as the freer hand given to the

Royal Ulster Constabulary during interrogation led to allegations of brutality and criticisms from Amnesty International that led to the subsequent Bennett Inquiry.[33] More embarrassingly, in 1978, the European Court of Human Rights found against the British government for its treatment of detainees in Northern Ireland. The withdrawal of special category status from political prisoners also prompted resistance from within the prisons, which in turn was to be the focus of continued opposition to British rule in Northern Ireland throughout the island of Ireland and the wider Irish diaspora.

A significant minority of Labour MPs and constituency activists had opposed bi-partisanship and the PTA, while many were supporters of TOM. Labour's return to opposition coincided with a rise in political activism around the issue of republican political prisoners, and gave rise to an outpouring of frustration directed against the previous administration's policy towards Ireland. In 1980, this tendency of the party formed the Labour Committee on Ireland—a response, in part, to the party leadership's attempt to limit debate on Ireland at the Labour conference the previous year. In 1981, following the upsurge in sympathy for the hunger strikers amongst its activists, the Labour Party did adopt a policy of the unification of Ireland by consent (of the six counties) with Labour acting as persuader. This was to mark the height of pro-nationalist sentiment in the Labour Party, during which this position was subject to gradual erosion.[34] However, even this apparent peak must be seen in a wider perspective; when those on the Labour left did discuss Ireland they retained the party's almost characteristic concern for national prestige when discussing the issue of the immediate withdrawal of troops (an original position of TOM);[35] even radical MPs of that period, such as Peter Hain, warned against this as a utopian demand that would make a Labour government appear cowardly.[36]

Even amongst those on the revolutionary left, where the demand for an immediate withdrawal of troops from Ireland was supported by groups such as the Socialist Workers' Party (SWP), the relationship between the struggle for independence in Ireland and socialism in Britain had become inverted from the revolutionary tradition of Marx.[37] Revolutionaries in Britain were often highly critical of republicanism's use of terrorism and limited social programme, which they claimed had alienated the loyalist working class.[38] Groups such as Militant and the CPGB were heavily critical of what they considered the sectarianism of the Provisional IRA, and argued that the priority in Northern Ireland was to campaign for workers rather than national unity. For most in the British Labour movement, the conflict in Ireland remained a remote and forbidding subject.

It is perhaps appropriate that the Labour Party, having acted consistently to contain classical republicanism, should be in office to preside over its degeneration into an appendage of the Good Friday Agreement. The Labour Party leadership can be seen, therefore, as having neutralised opposition to the Partition of Ireland in 1921 by highlighting the need to defend the empire and, latterly, the rights of minorities. In 1949, the Labour leadership drafted a new Government of Ireland Act that enshrined Stormont's right to remain in the Union. From 1969 onward, the Labour leadership has sought (and supported) a bi-partisan approach to Northern Ireland that has sought to contain the impact of republican political violence. Between 1974 and 1979, the Labour government pursued its war against the IRA through a combined use of covert security operations and an ideological offensive to deprive republican prisoners of political legitimacy. The content of the policy remained the maintenance of Northern Ireland within the Union through 'normalisation'. From the zenith of Labour's support for the unification of Ireland by consent in 1981, Labour has returned to its traditional position of defence of the Union under 'New Labour' albeit through the rhetoric of respecting the diversity of traditions.

A renewed political offensive upon the welfare state and trade unionism from the Conservative governments in the 1980s created conditions which forced a major reassessment of what the Labour Party stood for; this was made manifest in the changes made to 'clause four' in 1995. The emergence of New Labour has, ironically, marked a return to Labour's traditional stance of defending the Union between Britain and Ireland.[39] Labour's 1997 manifesto carried references to the principle of consent and the reconciliation of the two traditions.

Labour's eighteen years in opposition were marked by profound change in the objectives of republicanism. Since 1986, the republican movement's tenets of political abstentionism have been gradually removed, initially with Sinn Fein's decision to participate in the 'Southern' *Daíl* and, ultimately, in the Northern Ireland Assembly. The current republican leadership has achieved wider acceptance and co-operation both domestically and internationally, whilst the unity of the movement has remained intact and its internal critics marginalised. These recent successes have come at the cost of the traditional stance of republicanism espoused in 1919 or 1969. Since 1992, and the launch of the document *Towards a Lasting Peace*, the republican movement has ceased to rely upon its own capacity to end partition and has instead sought to ally itself with 'persuaders' (constitutional nationalists in the North, the Irish government, and even the United States) to achieve its objectives. The IRA ceasefire of September 1994 and the 'complete cessation of military operations' in July 1997 have been called without any prospect of British withdrawal; the 1998 referenda, which endorsed the 'Good Friday Agreement', were held simultaneously within the respective parts of Ireland rather than one political unit, as republicans had always demanded. The willingness of the IRA to call two ceasefires with the prospect of the continuation of partition, coupled with the acceptance by Sinn Fein of junior partnership to the Dublin government and Constitutional Nationalists, and an increased emphasis by them upon their electoral mandate within the 'North', even to the yielding up of arms by the IRA, indicates that Irish republicanism has shared in the change that has overtaken many of the former national liberation struggles since 1989.[40] The current Labour administration has inherited a situation in which a fundamental change in the character of the republican movement had already become apparent; there are still republicans, but no republicanism.

Notes

1. G. Bell, *Troublesome Business: The Labour Party and the Irish question* (London, 1982), p.150.
2. W. Thompson, *The Long Death of British Labourism: Interpreting a political culture* (London, 1993), p.16.
3. Troops Out Movement, *Tom–Tom: Bulletin of the Troops Out Movement* (London, 1975), p.2.
4. D. Fernbach (ed.), *Marx: The First International and after* (London, 1974), p.169.
5. V. I. Lenin, *The Nascent Trend of Imperialist Economism* (London, 1969 edn), p.31.
6. ibid., p.66.
7. Thompson, *British Labourism*, p.86.
8. ibid., p.14.
9. J. Loughlin, *Ulster Unionism and British National Identity since 1885* (London, 1995), p.5.
10. Bell, *Troublesome Business*, p.29.
11. Loughlin, *Ulster Unionism*, p.73.
12. ibid., p.52.
13. Bell, *Troublesome Business*, p.43.
14. D. Reed, *Ireland: The key to British revolution* (Dublin, 1984) p.71.
15. Bell, *Troublesome Business*, p.60.
16. ibid., p.67.
17. ibid., p.85.
18. Loughlin, *Ulster Unionism*, p.158.
19. ibid., p.152.
20. R. Purdie, 'Friends of Ireland: British Labour and Irish Nationalism, 1945–49' in T. Gallagher and J. (eds), *Contemporary Irish Studies* (Manchester, 1983), p.86.
21. G. Bing, *John Bull's Other Ireland* (London, 1950), p.1.

22. ibid., p.18.
23. Purdie, 'Friends of Ireland', p.89.
24. ibid., p.88.
25. P. Bew and H. Patterson, *The British State and the Ulster Crisis: From Wilson to Thatcher* (London, 1985), p.19.
26. Reed, *Ireland*, p.177.
27. T. P. Coogan, *The IRA* (London, 2000), p.345.
28. Bew and Patterson, *British State*, p.23.
29. Bell, *Troublesome Business*, p.115.
30. J. Loughlin, *Ulster Unionism*, p.186.
31. ibid.
32. Bew and Patterson, *British State*, p.91.
33. Loughlin, *Ulster Question*, p.81.
34. N. Randall, 'New Labour and Northern Ireland', in D. Coates and P. Lawler (eds), *New Labour in Power* (Manchester, 2000), p.92.
35. Thompson, *Long Death*, p.76.
36. Labour Committee on Ireland, *Labour and Ireland* (London, 1980), p.6.
37. Socialist Workers' Party, *Why we say Troops Out of Ireland!* (London, 1980), p.14.
38. ibid., p.13.
39. Randall, 'New Labour', p.93.
40. M. Ryan, *War and Peace in Ireland: Britain and the IRA in the new world order* (London, 1994), p.41.

Property, Economic Interest and the Configuration of Rural Conflict in Sixteenth and Seventeenth-Century England

Stephen Hipkin

> At a certain stage of development the material productive forces of society come into conflict with the existing relations of production or—this merely expresses the same thing in legal terms—with the property relations within the framework of which they have operated hitherto...The changes in the economic foundation lead sooner or later to the transformation of the whole immense superstructure. In studying such transformations it is always necessary to distinguish between the material transformation of the economic conditions of production, which can be determined with the precision of natural science, and the legal, political, religious, artistic or philosophic—in short, ideological forms in which men become conscious of this conflict and fight it out. Just as one does not judge an individual by what he thinks about himself, so one cannot judge such a period of transformation by its consciousness.
>
> Karl Marx, *Preface to the Critique of Political Economy* (1859)

Complex and intriguing though the long debate has been, what follows is not intended to add to the gallons of ink that have been consumed in attempts to clarify what, precisely, Marx was arguing when he summarised the 'general conclusion...which, once reached, became the guiding principle of my studies'. What does seem clear, however, is that whatever else he intended to convey, Marx understood societies to be structured by classes defined by reference to objective relations of production (legally sanctioned as property relations), rather than by reference to class *consciousness*. Somewhat unfashionably, this article is concerned with the analysis of class structure in the sense that I take Marx to have understood the concept, as something that exists willy-nilly wherever antagonistic relations of production obtain. When historians conclude, as they overwhelmingly do, that Tudor and Stuart England was not a class society, they usually mean that it was not a self-consciously class society. To the extent that this was the case, the challenge is to explain why it was the case. I shall suggest that insofar as the development of a consistent sense of class consciousness and identity *was* inhibited in the fields, forests and villages of early modern England, this was a consequence of the sheer complexity and mutability of the configurations of class interest that existed in many rural localities by the late Elizabethan period, and of the fact that diversified resource-generating strategies frequently, and often simultaneously, placed individuals at different points on the spectrum of relations of production.

The starting point for our investigation of pre-industrial class structure is the justly celebrated essay originally published in 1976, in which Robert Brenner sought, *inter alia*, to challenge the prevailing demographic determinism that he held responsible for:

> a heroically simplified version of developments before the nineteenth century in which the long-term movements in prices, in income distribution, in investment, in real wages, and in migration are dominated by changes in the growth of population.[1]

Brenner did this not by the common historian's resort to chipping away at the walls of received orthodoxy, but by aiming a wrecking-ball at the entire edifice. The problem with the thesis that population change provides the key to explaining European economic development in the medieval and early modern periods is, he argued, quite simply that similar demographic trends could be accompanied by 'dramatically contrasting trends of economic development'. So, for example, in France, as population increased during the sixteenth and seventeenth centuries, 'there was extreme fragmentation of (land)holdings and declining productivity', whereas in England a parallel growth of population was accompanied by the consolidation of holdings which were farmed out to large tenant farmers who, in turn, cultivated them with the aid of wage labour. 'Accompanying this change in the organisation of production were major increases in agricultural productivity, with truly epoch making results'. While much of continental Europe was gripped by violent price fluctuations and crises of subsistence during the late seventeenth and early eighteenth centuries, England enjoyed stable population and low agricultural prices, which released spending power 'throughout the middle and perhaps even the lower class so as to expand the home market and fuel the steady growth of industry into the period of the industrial revolution'.[2]

If the demographic model could not explain the divergent development of England and France, Brenner was quite clear about where enlightenment should be sought. In order fully to comprehend long-term economic developments, growth and/or retrogression in the late medieval and early modern period, it is critical to analyse the relatively autonomous processes by which particular class structures, especially property or surplus-extraction relations, are established, and in particular the class conflicts to which they do (or do not) give rise. For it is in the outcome of such class conflicts—the reaffirmation of the old property relations or their destruction and the consequent establishment of a new structure—that is to be found perhaps the key to the problem of long-term economic development in late-medieval and early modern Europe.[3]

In concrete terms, the argument Brenner advanced with respect to English economic development may be briefly summarised as follows. In England, as throughout most of Western Europe in the immediate wake of the Black Death, the balance of power in the class struggle between lords and serfs shifted heavily in favour of the latter. The peasantry were able to exploit the labour shortages caused by epidemic mortality and, by dint of flight and resistance, successfully broke feudal controls over their mobility and personal freedom. The crucial determinant of the subsequent path of English economic development was the failure of the English peasantry to consolidate the gains they had made by the mid-fifteenth century by winning 'full and essentially freehold control over their customary tenements'. Brenner offered two reasons for this failure. First, demographic collapse in the late-fourteenth and fifteenth centuries left vacant many former customary peasant holdings, which landlords simply added to their demesnes, thereby 'significantly reducing the area of land which potentially could be subjected to essentially peasant proprietorship'.[4] Second, although rent on customary land was 'fixed by custom',[5] and thus of dwindling value in the face of inflation,

> one crucial loophole often remained open to those landlords who sought to undermine the freehold-tending claims of the customary tenants who still remained on their lands and clung to their holdings. They could insist on the right to charge fines at will whenever peasant land was conveyed—that is, in sales or on inheritance. Indeed, in the end entry fines often appear to have provided the landlords with the lever they needed to dispose of customary peasant tenants, for in the long run fines could be substituted for competitive commercial rents…With the peasants' failure to establish essentially freehold control over the land, the landlords were able to engross, consolidate and enclose, to create large farms and to lease them to capitalist tenants who could afford to make capital investments.

Such investments, in turn, were 'made feasible through the development of a variety of different leaseholding arrangements, which embodied a novel form of landlord/tenant relationship'. In place of the 'traditionally antagonistic relationship in which landlord squeezing undermined tenant initiative' there emerged 'landlord/tenant symbiosis which brought mutual co-operation in investment and improvement', as tenants paying what Le Roy Ladurie dubbed 'capitalist rent', were 'assured that they could take a reasonable share of the increased revenue resulting from their capital investments and not have them confiscated by the landlords' rent increases'.[6]

Brenner's bold but essentially simple diagnosis of the determinants of the course of English economic development is history in a heroic style fit to match that of any demographic determinist.[7] And it is beyond doubt true that large-scale capitalist farms did emerge in England in precisely the manner that Brenner described. Lords did break customary tenancies, add them to their demesnes, engross, consolidate and enclose, thereby creating large farms which they then leased to capitalist tenants with whom they enjoyed a symbiotic and harmonious relationship. *Sometimes*. But an account of the emergence of *large-scale* capitalist farming is not the same thing as an analysis of the emergence of capitalist farming *per se*, and there were other English routes towards capitalist farming between the mid-fifteenth and the mid-eighteenth centuries, which, in their often-contested variety, produced a host of constellations of struggle and much tactical entertaining of strange bedfellows. In the final analysis, by mistaking one path for the only path out of the Malthusian cycle, Brenner succeeds only in substituting one heroically simplified version of English history for another.

Lords, peasants and property

Understandably enough, given his starting point, Brenner's identification of 'landlord' and 'peasant' classes is rooted in the property relations of the medieval manor, the former comprising manorial lords, the latter comprising serfs, and, once they had won their personal freedom, the tenants of manorial lords.[8] To the extent that this class specification continues to reflect *substantive* property relations during the early modern period, it remains relevant and useful. But Brenner was right to insist on the signal importance of the outcome of class conflict and the consequent reaffirmation or *destruction* of existing property relations (and *ipso facto* class relations) in determining the subsequent course of economic development. One major problem with his analysis, I want to suggest, lies in his partial misdiagnosis of the outcome of the class struggle between lords and peasants in the fifteenth and especially the sixteenth century.

The claim, upon which so much of Brenner's thesis hinges—that the English peasantry failed to 'establish essentially freehold control over the land' is true only in the sense that a *proportion* of the descendants of villeins failed to do so. Brenner did not deny this, but nor did he advertise the indications in the sources on which he relied (notably Kerridge) that manorial tenants who did secure 'essentially freehold control'—and hence became, in *substantive* terms, proprietors, comprised much more than a small minority.[9] The increasingly problematical nature of Brenner's model of class structure is, however, all too easily disguised by the essential continuity of *technical* descriptions of property relations in contemporary documentation since, throughout the early modern period, from the perspective of the manorial steward, *effective* proprietors remained technically manorial tenants just as *effective* tenants remained technically manorial tenants. To avoid the manifold confusions that often arise from the undifferentiated use of the term 'tenant' in descriptions of both technical and substantive property relationships, it is necessary clearly to distinguish between what may be termed proprietor-tenants and real-tenants.

Most obvious among proprietor-tenants in early modern England are freeholders. Virtually all manorial tenants in Kent held their land by common socage; that is, free or 'frank', as opposed to base tenure, and freeholders were also particularly common in East Anglia. Freeholders held both heritable estates (interests) and the right to alienate their land, (the two basic qualifications for property ownership), and such dues as they owed to the manorial lord (by virtue of which they remained technically manorial tenants) were fixed, for the most part nominal, and seldom if ever sufficient to threaten a freeholder's security of tenure. Manorial lords could do nothing to oust a freeholder. But a significant proportion of those with base tenures, that is, tenures held at the will of the lord according to the custom of the manor, also enjoyed security of tenure.[11]

The principal form of customary tenure that had emerged in succession to villeinage during the late medieval period was copyhold, so called because tenants held as title deeds certified copies of entries of their holdings and grants in the rolls of the manor courts. Great diversity was to be found among copyhold tenures, but the distinction which, *during the later sixteenth century* (though arguably not before), came to be recognised as of most import, lay between, on the one hand, copyholds for life or lives, and, on the other, copyholds of inheritance. Copyholders for life or lives held for fixed terms with no legally recognised right of renewal. In other words, although possessing what was strictly a customary tenure, they held what was in substance a form of leasehold. At the expiry of the last life, a landlord wishing to reorganise the manorial estate was entirely free to refuse to grant a new copy and to add the land to the demesne. Copyholders for lives were also vulnerable because even if the lord was willing to grant another copy, the absence of any custom limiting the amount of the renewal fine left them exposed to financial exploitation as rising population increased competition for land. Thus in Dorset, where the majority of copyholders held for lives, entry fines on most manors rose steeply between 1570 and 1670. On the earl of Salisbury's estates in the Cranborne area the average fine rose from 10s. per acre in 1571, to £2. 1s. in 1640, a four-fold increase, compared with a three-fold increase in wheat prices over the same period. Copyholders for life or lives therefore lacked 'essentially freehold control over the land' and, as real-tenants in a competitive climate for holdings, were vulnerable in exactly the way Brenner described. Such copyholds were the dominant form of customary tenure in western England, but in the eastern half of the country 'the usual customary tenure was copyhold of inheritance, as it was also in Taunton Deane, the Cheshire cheese country and the Lancashire Plain'; indeed it has been estimated that about half of all copyholders held on such terms.[11]

Copyhold of inheritance and, in northern England, tenant right, were forms of landholding in which local customary precedent served to protect the tenants' right to inherit (and alienate) their land. Nevertheless, following Tawney's lead, Brenner sought to argue that many copyholders of inheritance did not begin to establish a freehold estate in their land until 'very late in the day—after a century of rising prices and rents'. Crucial in this regard is the question of entry fines. Where copyholders of inheritance could prove a custom of fixed and certain fines they were safe, and the lord's real income from his lands was progressively devalued, but, Brenner claimed, where fines were 'arbitrary', manorial lords were able to overcome the freehold-tending claims of tenants simply by raising fines to a level beyond the means of an heir. Until the equity courts developed the doctrine that fines on heritable copyholds, though 'arbitrary', must be reasonable, that is, not so great as to defeat a copyhold of inheritance, tenants of heritable copyholds without fixed fines were no more secure than copyholders for lives, or demesne leaseholders.[12] Since Kerridge had offered no evidence of Chancery setting 'reasonable' maxima for fines prior to 1586, Brenner assumed that the doctrine of reasonableness was late sixteenth century in origin, and thus 'late in the day'. He assumed, equally, that lords had been busily exploiting the lack of it in order to oust heritable copyholds and effect conversions to leasehold throughout the sixteenth century, and that the copyholders of inheritance who had survived to the late sixteenth century 'must very often have been rather substantial figures, capable of paying the rising rents (in the form of higher fines) or buying up property themselves'.[13]

These assumptions have been effectively challenged by Hoyle, who points out, first, that 'pleadings asking the Chancellor to rule on fines had been brought to the court at least a generation before' 1586; secondly, that there are no data with which to compare the quantity of copyhold of inheritance at the beginning and end of the sixteenth century; and finally, that Brenner credits lords with 'an unreasonable degree of foresight', since it was 'far from obvious in the mid-sixteenth century that England was entering on a half century of rising agricultural prosperity'. There are, indeed, examples of lords *creating* hereditary copyholds during the early Tudor period. Where conversions of heritable copyholds to leaseholds did occur before 1550, Hoyle suggests, they were probably motivated by lords wishing to anticipate income while stopping short of selling capital assets, since the beneficial lease that replaced the copy brought in an initial fine. Copyholders of inheritance were prepared to accept this 'as a premium paid to avoid having to find other fines during the period of the term', and because 'in itself the lease did nothing to discourage the belief that tenant land was hereditary land', since they, like lords, based decisions on experience, and recent experience was that lords were keen to hang on to tenants. Conversions of heritable copyholds to leaseholds were uncontentious in the early and mid-sixteenth century 'because the characteristic advantages of leasehold to the lord then lay in the future'; lords who initiated them had the gift of good fortune rather than of foresight. However, 'once the economic advantages of conversion became obvious, those lords who tried to break tenure or raise fines found their tenants had good reasons to resist their overtures and stood in a relatively strong position with the backing of the equity courts'. Under these circumstances, apart from doing nothing, lords often had little choice but to buy out their copyholders' interest (if and when they were willing to sell) or else to raise money by selling confirmations of custom or the freehold title to the copyholders themselves.[14]

Thus, even as population increase created a buoyant demand for holdings in sixteenth-century England, a significant proportion of copyhold tenancies, perhaps even a majority, remained in the hands of proprietor-tenants who were invulnerable to the kind of direct assault by manorial lords that Brenner saw as a crucial determinant of the subsequent path of English economic development. Tenants on the island of Portland, for example, enjoyed heritable copyholds with rents certain at 3d. per acre and fines fixed at one year's rent, and they had ample rights of common grazing and stone-quarrying, while in the Lea valley, fifteen miles north of

London, mean rents on heritable copyhold arable stood at just 10d. per acre in the 1590s, only 3d. more than in the 1530s, while entry fines rose by just 5s. per acre over the same period. *Leasehold* rents, by contrast, increased rapidly from the 1540s. Tenants-at-will (i.e. those with no legal claim on the land beyond the right safely to harvest crops they had put into the ground) suffered particularly as landlords exploited their insecurity. On one sub-manor in Cheshunt, the average rent for 14 tenants with arable land in the open fields was raised from 9d. to 2s. 6d. per acre in 1545–6, and, at the same time, rents for enclosed arable croft rose from 2s. 9d. to 6s. 3d. per acre, and those for meadow from 3s. 6d. to 8s. per acre.[15]

The alteration of *effective* property relations between manorial lords and that proportion of tenants who achieved security of tenure directly implies that an unamended taxonomy of class conflict—manorial landlord versus manorial tenant—remains appropriate for the early modern period, at best, only when and where tenants did not exercise proprietory control over holdings. Even then, as we shall see, it is frequently inadequate to describe the structure of social relations in the countryside. The migration of a considerable number of manorial tenants into the ranks of *de facto* landowners during the fifteenth and sixteenth centuries, was, unsurprisingly, accompanied by a reconfiguration of their economic interest and options.

'Rise of the English yeoman'

One option for the proprietor-tenant, plainly, was subsistence farming. But the inability of manorial lords greatly to augment rents from the holdings of proprietor-tenants also allowed those who chose directly to farm their holdings, and who were able and willing to produce a marketable surplus in excess of that needed simply to sustain the family farm, to pocket much of the increasing income they obtained from rising agricultural prices. This they were then able to deploy in the hire or purchase of additional holdings and in measures to improve productivity. Real-tenants, by contrast, were vulnerable to sharp rent increases when their terms expired. That said, until the later-sixteenth century some real-tenants *also* had the chance to accumulate capital, since, in their efforts to attract tenants during the era before agricultural prices began to take off, manorial lords had often been willing to grant demesne leaseholds at low rents for very long terms (80 years was not uncommon). Furthermore, purchasers of ex-monastic property after the 1530s often found it 'encumbered by very long leases which the abbots had granted in their last days often in order to make as much as possible out of fines before they were dispossessed by the king'.[16] Whether underpinned by freehold, heritable copyhold or long-lease tenure, the enhanced opportunities for capital accumulation presented to and seized by some tenants (and rejected by others) helped speed the process of differentiation within the ranks of the peasantry that is most commonly celebrated as the 'rise of the English yeoman'. Armed with the capital that manorial lords had been prevented from pocketing in rent, *some* tenants, on their own initiative, were able to build up sizeable commercial farms; *pace* Brenner, the process was by no means *always* seigneurially driven.[17] Indeed in some regions—Romney Marsh is a notable example—manorial lords did next to nothing to sponsor the development of larger farms.[18]

But there was another option. As befitted those who were in the nature of landed proprietors, freeholders and copyholders of inheritance did not have to farm their land in order to accumulate capital, they could easily turn landlord. Freeholders were entirely at liberty to let, or, from the perspective of the manor, sublet their holdings to whomsoever and on whatever terms they chose.[19] Manorial custom usually allowed copyholders of inheritance to sublet without licence for terms of three years, and licences for longer terms (on payment of a small fine) were, it appears, rarely refused. But large numbers of real-tenants could also take the rentier option. Subletting was widely permitted by the terms agreed between landlords and indentured lessees, and custom on manors with copyholders for lives usually permitted the copyholder to let his or her holdings for a year and a day without licence. In some places manorial custom made subletting even easier. At Edgmond in Shropshire the copyholder could sublet for three successive terms of three years without licence, and at Winsham and Purtlington in the far West of Dorset, manorial custom was 'that "every tenant in possession dwelling within this manor may have undertenants without the lord's licence"'. Elsewhere, where custom was more restrictive, manorial tenants were sufficiently interested in playing the rentier to test the boundaries, 'trying to read into the customs the right to lease without licence', and pressing the issue in land suits.[20]

How widespread were subtenancies in early modern England? Kerridge found that 'nearly all records of manorial courts in the early modern period abound with entries of subtenancy licences, presentments for not obtaining licences and references to undertenants, "undersettles" and inmates'. These, he argued, furnish 'impressive evidence of a profusion of copyhold undertenancies', the more so given that subleases for a year or less required no licence. Other historians have been similarly impressed. Joan Thirsk found 'widespread' subletting in five early seventeenth-century Lincolnshire manors, Tupling concluded that 'a quite considerable amount of land was being let to subtenants' in Rossendale (Lancashire), and

Spufford's examination of will evidence led to her discovery of an 'army of subtenants' in the Cambridgeshire village of Willingham. Probate material suggests another early-seventeenth century army of manorial subtenants in the rural hinterland of Faversham. So struck was Kerridge by the evidence indicating a vigorous market in 'subtenancies and sublettings of demesne, socage and customary lands' in sixteenth and seventeenth-century England that he concluded that contemporaries 'generally recognised' that they were 'occupied largely by subtenants'.[21] No historian, to my knowledge, has directly disputed this claim.

Yet if textbooks formally acknowledge the possible scale of subletting, the problem remains that the proportion of land in the occupation of manorial subtenants in any given place at any given time is not usually susceptible to accurate measurement. The principal sources capable of yielding synchronic quantitative data for those interested in the structure of landholding are manorial and estate surveys, of which thousands survive, but 'in commissioning a survey of his manors, the lord was solely concerned with tenants who held of him and not with their subtenants'. Of the latter, the surveys usually tell us little or nothing.[22] So, if Kerridge's impressionistic conclusion about what contemporaries 'generally recognised' is accurate, a major and unpalatable implication is that although manorial surveys remain sound indicators of the size and distribution of tenancies held directly of the lord, the majority may be hopelessly inaccurate guides to the structure of *farming* in early modern England: as inaccurate as a register of property owners would be as a guide to the population of a village.

In the minority of cases in which manorial surveys *do* indicate subtenancies it is usually because the formal tenant had made his or her lessee responsible for the payment of rent to the lord of the manor, and the name was recorded for the convenience of the rent collector. What is revealed is often striking. At Bedfont, of 140 freehold parcels surveyed c.1546, 46 were occupied by their tenants (that is, in effect, owner-occupied) and 93 by subtenants. Of the 25 freeholdings surveyed in Rhode borough in the hundredal manor of Faversham in 1608 at least ten were sublet, 49 of the 89 holdings on four west Kent manors in 1642 were sublet, and early land tax assessments for the Kent parishes of Meopham, Monkton and Eastry indicate that during the 1690s between 60 per cent and 80 per cent of holdings were in the hands of subtenants. More arresting still, the chance survival of a fieldbook naming both the manorial tenants, mainly copyholders of inheritance, *and* their sub-tenants on the manor of Cannock in Staffordshire in 1554 reveals that of 1,400 acres in enclosures, just '510 acres (36 per cent) remained in the hands of the tenants, and 890 acres (64 per cent) were sublet'. Among the 52 tenants, no less than 16 lived away from the manor and sublet *all* their land, their holdings varying in size from a single cottage to 223 acres. Conversely, half of all those *farming* on the manor (37) occupied land *entirely* by virtue of subtenancies, while some manorial tenants with smallholdings 'increased the size of their farms out of all proportion through subtenanting'. One man held nine acres as a manorial tenant, of which he leased out eight acres, but farmed over 200 acres as a subtenant, and the largest farmer on the manor, who cultivated 278 acres, occupied 91 of them as a tenant and 187 acres as a subtenant.[23] But perhaps the most spectacular and sustained evidence thus far unearthed for (from the manorial perspective) farming by subtenants in early modern England is contained within the surviving records of local taxes levied on land occupiers within the Romney Marsh region between the late-sixteenth and mid-nineteenth centuries. By the mid-seventeenth century, '85 per cent of the 23,000 acres in the Level of Romney Marsh was in the hands of the lessees and sublessees of demesne lands, and the lessees, or *occasionally* the sublessees, of socage lands (i.e. subtenants, or occasionally their undertenants, using Kerridge's terminology)'. A century later, in 1768, less than one acre in every 12 across the 43,000 acres of the Romney Marsh region was actually being farmed by its manorial tenant. Henry Nickoll's 624-acre farm comprised 10.5 acres of owner-occupied land, and 613.5 acres leased from no less than 14 different freeholders, in parcels ranging in size from half an acre to 143 acres.[24] At the very least, it seems safe to conclude that subletting of manorial tenancies and demesne leaseholds was taking place on a significant scale in early modern England.

Farming logistics often led manorial tenants to lease out some of their own holdings in order to rent more conveniently located land, but it is not difficult to see why a good proportion, both among those who purchased and among those who inherited copyholds and freeholds, treated their holdings as capital assets often best deployed in the leasehold market. As rentiers, proprietor-tenants could reap the benefit of rising rent values that their security of tenure had denied to their own manorial lords. Thus the farmers who actually worked these holdings were placed under the pressures of competitive rents, as Brenner thought, *but not by whom he thought*. It was a section of Brenner's 'peasant' class, or at least their descendants, rather than his landlord class, who, in these circumstances, were doing the squeezing. Where copyhold tenants on holdings in Rossendale were paying rents of 1s. 4d., 2s. 9^1/2d. and 4d. to the manorial lord, the subtenants farming *the same holdings* were paying rents to the copyholder of 4s., 7s. 2^1/2d., and 9s. 4d. respectively. On the manor of Accrington, while the lord received 2^1/2d. and

4d. for two holdings from the copyholder, the copyholder was receiving 13s. 11^{1}/$_{2}$d. and 43s. 11d. respectively from the subtenant. In 1500, the London goldsmith Henry Coote, an absentee copyholder on the manor of Cheshunt, was receiving £31. 10s. 10d. from his subtenants, almost seven times the £4 12s. 6d. Coote was paying out to the lord of Cheshunt manor.[25] Absentee manorial lords in all parts of the country leased demesnes to tenants whose sole intention was to make a margin by subletting. Where the burden of the demesne lease was placed up-front in the entry fine, as was common in western England and where the manorial lord was an ecclesiastical or other corporate body, demesne lessees with the necessary ready capital might thereafter make handsome profits from subletting in smaller parcels (which commanded a premium) at rack rents.[26] In 1577, the demesne leasehold of the archiepiscopal manor of Boughton-under-Blean (some 806 acres) came into the hands of John Parker (son of Matthew, Elizabeth's first archbishop!) who subsequently sublet it for an annual rent of £168, more than three times the rent owed to the archbishop.[27]

Of course, none of the above should be taken to imply that tenants enjoying heritable estates were invulnerable during the later sixteenth and early seventeenth centuries. Death, disease, harvest failure and a host of other individual misfortunes conduced to the sales and surrenders of freehold and heritable copyhold land that manorial landlords could not deliberately effect by dramatic hikes in entry fines.[28] The impact of partible inheritance customs, whether in the form of increasing financial burdens on the family farm in favour of younger children, or in the direct division of holdings, particularly threatened the long-term security of freeholders and copyholders of inheritance with fixed fines, *precisely because* it was on tenancies whose financial liabilities to landlords were least burdensome that successive generations of tenants were able to allow sub-division to advance furthest. In so doing they often sacrificed long-term security on the altar of providing some landed interest for each male heir. In Kent, the custom of gavelkind and adherence to its principles among will-makers below the wealthiest ranks of rural society not only produced dispersed and fragmented ownership, but also contributed to the very active market in land sales that is reflected, for instance, in the fact that of 90 surnames appearing in the list of freeholders in Boughton manor compiled by parliamentary commissioners in 1647, only 25 can be found in the manorial survey carried out in 1570.[29] Nevertheless, although this is not the place to consider post-Restoration trends, it is reasonable to suggest that the position of smaller legally secure proprietor-tenants was also *practically* much more secure in the era before population expansion ground to a halt in the 1650s and brought about the sea-change in the economic climate that was to result in a century of depressed agricultural prices and rents.[30]

When freehold and customary tenancies came on the market during the sixteenth and seventeenth centuries they attracted buyers from across the social spectrum, and wherever freehold and copyhold land was to be found, so were tenants who held land by both tenures. Spratt's finding that over half the land on a group of early seventeenth-century Norfolk and Suffolk manors was in the possession of tenants who were both freeholders and copyholders probably reflects the situation throughout East Anglia and a number of other regions. Radical agitators in the 1640s and 1650s may have campaigned for the transformation of copyholds into freeholds on the grounds that copyhold was a servile and degrading tenure, but few if any were deterred from acquiring it on that account. Denzil Holles, the younger son of a peer and a prominent parliamentarian leader in the House of Commons during the 1640s, was a copyhold tenant of the earl of Salisbury at Damerham. A century later, Earl Cowper possessed copyholds in a number of Hertfordshire manors, by dint of which he was tenant to a fellow peer *and* to one undistinguished country squire. It has been suggested that by the eighteenth century, 'particularly in the western counties of the kingdom, many of the lesser gentry depended very heavily upon income from land held by copy or 99-year leases determinable upon lives, and some owned little freehold, or none at all'. Urban dwellers ranging from modest craftsmen to wealthy merchants likewise invested in copyhold. In short, many copyholders were in no sense peasants, they were not even the descendants of peasants.[31]

Complex property relations

Clearly then, students of rural society in early modern England must expect to encounter a great diversity of mutable configurations of substantive property relations. Certainly, large numbers of manorial freeholds and heritable copyholds were owned and worked by subsistence farmers.[32] But their proprietors also included commercial farmers, urban artisans and merchants, gentry, and peers of the realm. The lord of one manor might be a copyholder on another. The proprietor-tenant of a copyhold might well hold, in any combination, additional copyholds, freeholds, demesne-leaseholds or tenancies at will on the same or other manors, and he or she might farm all or part of these holdings while leasing out others. In turn, *farming* enterprises could be assembled from land held from manorial lords by any combination of copyhold, freehold, leasehold or at-will tenures, but the farmer actually cultivating the soil might hold much or all of his or her land not as a manorial tenant or demesne leaseholder, but as the subtenant of manorial tenants and demesne-leaseholders. A farmer might therefore have any number of landlords and yet no landlord at all, and be paying market-driven rack rents to proprietor-tenant rentiers whose own fiscal liabilities to manorial lords were wholly immune to market forces. To describe these scenarios is not to chronicle the extremes of what was theoretically possible but rarely occurred. In more or less complex manifestations they were commonplace in early modern England.

But property in land was of two kinds; holdings, and rights of common in fields, meadows and wastes, and for many freeholders and copyholders the latter was the more vital property. By the mid-nineteenth century, of course, common rights on arable land had been virtually eliminated, those on pasture largely extinguished, and farming was carried out under conditions of exclusive ownership. This transformation was the product of enclosure, and, although there were significant regional variations, it occurred most rapidly during the seventeenth century, before the era of parliamentary legislation.[33] Viewed objectively and in overall terms, it is undeniable that the exercise of rights of common on unimproved wastes and on arable fields after harvest did restrict the possibilities for commercial farming, and that engrossment, consolidation and physical enclosure did facilitate 'significant agrarian advance'. But that does not mean that capitalist farms could not develop on the back of the exploitation of common right, or that we can equate resistance to enclosure with resistance to capitalist agriculture or capitalist definitions of property rights. When, in 1602, the Canterbury merchant and local freeholder John Sutton gave evidence in Star Chamber about his role in resisting the enclosure of Denstroud common, he explained that he wished to uphold the right of common 'belonging or appurtenant' to some of his land, a property asset which, as it happened, generated revenue for Sutton by being sublet. What was at stake in this and numerous similar confrontations was not an ideological fissure between capitalist and anti-capitalist notions of property rights, but rather the mutually exclusive claims arising from, on the one hand, the private ownership of land and, on the other, the private ownership of use-rights on the same land.[34] The gradual extirpation of right of common between the sixteenth and the nineteenth centuries was the product as much of the rationalisation as of the emergence of capitalism in the countryside.

Few in early modern England, least of all commercial farmers, stood on high to champion the cause of efficient capitalist organisation *per se*, they judged from the perspective of immediate interest, and where the immediate interest of commercial farmers did not favour enclosure they opposed it. In forest and fenland areas, in particular, the interest of many yeomen and gentry was best served within the context of regional agrarian specialisation by their ability to over-exploit waste and commons. The seventeenth century may have seen a great deal of enclosure, much of it ostensibly 'by agreement', but in South-west England, in the forest of Dean, and in the Lincolnshire and Cambridgeshire fens, the enclosure and drainage schemes of crown projectors met persistent and widespread resistance from gentry and middling sort yeomen, as well as from subsistence farmers.[35] There has been much disagreement about which of these groups *led* resistance to enclosure, but the debate rather obscures the crucial points. First, there were subsistence *and* profit-making agenda amongst the opponents of the crown projectors, and secondly, notwithstanding the disparate wider affiliations and agenda of those participating in the theatre of riot, opposition to enclosure could still produce a broad-based federation of convenience to defend a mutual interest in right of common.

At an individual level, interest might dictate opposition to enclosure in one context, and support for it in others. Thus, in 1582, wearing the hat of a paternalist justice of the peace, we find Sir Michael Sondes of Throwley in Kent rounding on the enclosure of Davington Green. It was, he declared, motivated by 'covetous and greedy desire', and 'no small annoyance to the common and public weal…a wicked act', an affront 'towards those poor members of the weal public that are injuriously wronged'. Twenty years later, wearing the hat of a man who had just purchased a 99-year lease on a large tract of woodland ripe for 'improvement', the same Sondes made two attempts unilaterally to enclose Denstroude common, 'to the end to shut off the commoners from their common'. The late-Elizabethan merchant oligarchs of Rye in Sussex bewailed the impact on the town's harbour, and trade, of drainage schemes in the Rother levels, but could not resist the urge to improve their own holdings in the vicinity. The Verney family had no doubts about the benefits of enclosure, and, having bought out all the small freeholds, relocated the leaseholds, and extinguished common rights on the waste, they finally enclosed the last of the common fields at Middle Claydon in Buckinghamshire in 1655. Meanwhile they bought a few acres and grazing rights in neighbouring Steeple Claydon, by virtue of which they were able to delay its enclosure for 120 years, thus limiting the amount of enclosed land available on the local market and maximising rents at Middle Claydon.[36]

As in forest regions elsewhere in England, Sir Michael Sondes's attempts to impose enclosure at Denstroude succeeded in mobilising opposition from a broad coalition of manorial tenants and their lessees, ranging from gentry and yeomen to very modest smallholders, united by their possession of common right, and operating in functional if not ideological alliance with those exercising marginal use-rights in the waste. In other circumstances, however, shared claims to right of common were themselves the origin of conflict. Particularly in areas where population densities were high and manorial waste was in short supply, right of common was under pressure not only from lords, or lessees acting with their approval, who wished to enclose, but also from the weight of competition amongst those seeking to graze their animals. Here, the struggle over access to pasture and other valuable use-rights pitched those defending a subsistence income against those whose right of common was a source of capital accumulation, and, *pari passu*, liberal, commonwealth aspirations to social inclusiveness against hard-headed appeals to custom-as-contract. It is, however, important to acknowledge also the *limited* extent to which fundamentally contrasting ideologies with respect to property were at stake in such struggles. Not many even among the more extravagant appeals to social inclusiveness were based on notions wholly inimical to 'capitalist definitions of property rights'. The claim, rehearsed in a case arising from Theberton in Suffolk in 1772, that 'everybody in the world may cut rushes on the common' was one, but the 're-ification of usages into properties' commenced as soon as use-rights began to be codified in court roll or popular memory, for at that point they became, necessarily, subject to exclusive claims by qualifying members of defined groups. Stephen Gateward's championing of the use-rights of the poor at Stixwold in Lincolnshire in 1607 was grounded upon the customary claims of 'inhabitants'; broadly inclusive, yes, but not quite 'everybody in the world'.[37]

Disputes amongst claimants to right of common were, then, not about the principle of exclusivity, but about degrees. Nonetheless, when the marginal poor, 'mere inhabitants', and squatters on manorial wastes appealed for tolerance of their exercise of use-rights, they did pose moral challenges. Occasionally they succeeded in winning support from those whose exercise of similar rights rested on much more strictly defined and elaborately buttressed contractual customary claims. Such was the case at Caddington common in the northern Chilterns during the later 1630s, where resistance to enclosure was led by 'increasingly gentrified' commoners who stood to be compensated if they cashed in their own legally watertight common rights, but who nonetheless defended the use-rights of the parish poor in the belief that 'the removal of common rights would inevitably lead to an increase in the burden of poverty and, in turn, of poor rates'. Elsewhere, more predictably, the poor would-be commoner got short shrift. When the labourer William Austen, claiming to follow the lead of many poor people, erected a cottage on Longbridge Lees, part of the manor of Conningbrook near Ashford, it was pulled down by freeholders who, as they subsequently explained in Star Chamber, regarded the erection of cottages by the poor (who then grazed animals on the common) as directly prejudicial to their rights of common on the Lees, and an encouragement to a great multitude to pester the parish. The freeholders of Conningbrook would have agreed with the judges' ruling, in Gateward's case, that right of common did not extend to those whose 'interest' extended no further than habitation, for 'such manner of interest the law will not suffer'.[38]

Unravelling economic interests

This paper will not have appealed to those who suppose it necessary to resort to scare quotes in order to refer to the 'real' world, or to post-modernists who imagine that what I imagine as real material economic interests with real effects are simply effects in my imagination. On the other hand, for socialist historians who remain sympathetic to the project of materialist Marxist analysis, and who have been less than impressed by the re-branding of the speculations of bishop Berkeley as space-age semiotics, the analysis of class structure remains the necessary if not sufficient foundation upon which any sound appreciation of forms and modalities of historical consciousness must be based. Here it has been argued that senses of class identity and class consciousness in early modern rural England were often fleeting and fragmentary, and were so because, both sequentially and simultaneously, many people derived their income in a variety of technically distinct class capacities; as owner-occupier, as rentier, as tenant, as sub-tenant, as wage-labourer, as propertied or habitation claimant to right of common, and so on.[39] In order to understand the often complex temporary alliances that were forged in all manner of resource-allocation disputes, there is no alternative to the difficult and painstaking task of unravelling the range and nature of economic interests at stake, interests that were invariably structured in the last instance by context-specific property relations.[40] Historians unacquainted with Marx's work (albeit often wilfully so) may be forgiven for entertaining the notion that class society can only be said to exist when class identity is a crucial, or rather *the* crucial component of contemporary cognitive experience. It is less easy to understand the persistence of the same assumption implicit in a great deal of avowedly Marx-influenced writing about the late-eighteenth and nineteenth centuries.[41] The existence of class structure no more depends upon the existence of class consciousness than the existence of the table depends upon knowledge of its existence. Those minded to disagree are welcome to their fantasies, and to their historical fictions.

Notes

1. R. Brenner, 'Agrarian class structure and economic development in pre-industrial Europe', in T.H. Aston and C.H.E. Philpin (eds), *The Brenner Debate: agrarian class structure and economic development in pre-industrial Europe* (Cambridge, 1987), p.13, (quoting H.J. Habbakkuk).
2. ibid., pp.23–4, 51–2, 54.
3. ibid., p.12.
4. It has been pointed out that 'given what we know about conditions in the fifteenth century' (Brenner's) argument at this point is 'perverse. It assumes that lords were able to find tenants to take in land on lease at a time when we also know that lords were granting land on increasingly favourable terms—without fines, with rent reductions—because of the overall shortage of tenants.' R. W. Hoyle, 'Tenure and the land market in early modern England: or a late contribution to the Brenner debate', *Economic History Review*, XLIII (1990), p.5.
5. In fact rents were not *invariably* fixed by custom. M. Overton, *Agricultural Revolution in England: the transformation of the agrarian economy, 1500–1850* (Cambridge, 1996), p.34.
6. Brenner, 'Agrarian class structure', pp.46–51, 28.
7. Brenner's portrayal of the course of English economic development occupied but one corner of the canvas upon which he painted his picture of developments across Europe over the entire medieval and early modern periods, but the boldness and essential simplicity of the strokes is characteristic of the entire composition.
8. Defined by reference to property relations, as serfs, the peasantry were victims of *coercive* surplus extraction and, as manorial *tenants*, of uncapped surplus extraction (rent) by lords. Legally secure French tenants remain, for Brenner, '*peasant proprietors*', presumably because they were victims of arbitrary surplus extraction in the form of taxes imposed by the French monarchical state, rather than because they were *subsistence* producers. Non-Marxist historians offer a range of definitions of the term 'peasantry', some requiring peasants to be landowners, some counting only freeholders as landowners, and some requiring that families rather than individuals owned land. Others are content to use the term 'peasant' loosely to describe 'the subsistence oriented farmer'. Brenner, 'Agrarian class structure', pp.31–33, 54–8; Brenner, 'The agrarian roots of European capitalism', in Aston and Philpin, *The Brenner Debate*, pp.306–7; A. Macfarlane, *The Origins of English Individualism* (Oxford, 1978), passim; R. C. Allen, *Enclosure and the Yeoman: the agricultural development of the South Midlands 1450–1850* (Oxford, 1992), pp.81–3; C. Clay, *Economic Expansion and Social Change: England 1500–1700: Vol. 1, People, land and towns* (Cambridge, 1984), p.60.
9. Brenner, 'Agrarian class structure', p.47 n. 76; *Idem*, 'Agrarian roots', pp.295, 310 n.191. E. Kerridge, *Agrarian Problems in the Sixteenth Century and After* (London, 1969), pp.35–46.
10. S. Hipkin, 'Sitting on his penny rent: conflict and right of common in

Faversham Blean, 1595–1610', *Rural History*, vol. 11 (2000), p.9; *Idem*, 'Tenant farming and short-term leasing on Romney Marsh, 1587–1705', *Economic History Review*, vol. LIII, no. 4 (2000), p.647; C.W. Chalklin, *Seventeenth-century Kent* (Rochester, 1978), pp.46–9, 55–63; Clay, *Economic Expansion*, p.87. Kerridge, *Agrarian Problems*, p.35; M. Campbell, *The English Yeoman under Elizabeth and the Early Stuarts* (London, 1983), pp.113–18.
11. Kerridge, *Agrarian Problems*, pp.35–7; R. H. Tawney, *The Agrarian Problem in the Sixteenth Century* (London, 1912), pp.297–300; Clay, *Economic Expansion*, pp.87–89; R. W. Hoyle, 'Tenure on the Elizabethan estates' in R. W. Hoyle (ed.), *The Estates of the English Crown 1558–1640* (Cambridge, 1992), p.164; J. H. Bettey, 'Land tenure and manorial custom in Dorset, 1570–1670', *Southern History*, vol. 4 (1982), pp.46–8; Campbell, *English Yeoman*, pp.119–121. C. Clay, 'Landlords and estate management in England, 1640–1750', in C. Clay (ed.), *Rural Society: landowners, peasants and labourers, 1500–1750* (Cambridge, 1990), pp.330–1.
12. Brenner, 'Agrarian class structure', p.47 and n.76; *Idem*, 'Agrarian roots', pp.295–6; Tawney, *Agrarian Problem*, pp.296–7; Hoyle, 'Tenure', p.163; Campbell, *English Yeoman*, pp.147–53. In some areas, fines on copyhold of inheritance were certain on descent, but arbitrary at the will of the lord on alienation. Kerridge estimated that during the sixteenth century 'nearly half, but a somewhat dwindling proportion, of the copyholds of inheritance were subject to arbitrary fines at both descent and alienation or surrender'. Kerridge, *Agrarian Problems*, pp.38–9, 43.
13. ibid., p.39; Brenner, 'Agrarian class structure', p.47 n.76; *Idem*, 'Agrarian roots', p.296.
14. Hoyle, 'Tenure and the land market', pp.3–17.
15. Bettey, 'Land tenure', p.49; P. Glennie, 'In search of agrarian capitalism: manorial land markets and the acquisition of land in the Lea Valley c.1450– c.1560', *Continuity and Change*, vol. 3 (1988), pp.15–17; Kerridge, *Agrarian Problems*, pp.45–6, 86–7.
16. Clay, *Economic Expansion*, p.86.
17. P. Croot and D. Parker, 'Agrarian class structure and the development of capitalism: France and England compared', in Aston and Philpin (eds), *The Brenner Debate*, p.85–6. Responding to Croot and Parker's criticisms, Brenner acknowledged 'the emergence of a class of larger commercial farmers out of a process of economic differentiation of the peasantry', but reasserted his view that this was 'critically conditioned by the fact that…they had no choice but to respond to the rising market by competing with one another' and that 'this compulsion to compete was only the *result* of the fact that *they were separated from possession of the land*, thus deprived of direct (non-market) access to their means of subsistence, correlatively consigned to leasehold status, and, as a result, subjected to the system of competitive rents'. Brenner, 'Agrarian roots', pp.300–1. This argument is unconvincing on two counts: (a) it is factually inaccurate since, as we have seen, many yeomen *were* proprietor-tenants in legally secure possession of their land and (b) it assumes, perversely, that positive opportunities for capital

accumulation *could not* in themselves act as a stimulant to commercial production by proprietor-tenants and that, lacking the compulsion to do otherwise, they would always opt for subsistence farming. Had this been the case, Kent would have remained a medieval backwater throughout the early modern period. As it was, the county was the pre-eminent supplier of grain to the capital by the later sixteenth century, for which see F. J. Fisher, 'The development of the London food market 1540–1640', reprinted in E.M. Carus-Wilson (ed.), *Essays in Economic History*, vol. one (London, 1963), pp.135–51.

18. Hipkin, 'Tenant farming', pp.652–5; cf. Allen, *Enclosure and the Yeoman*, p.88.
19. Campbell, *English Yeoman*, pp.114–18; Kerridge, *Agrarian Problems*, p.48.
20. Equally, manorial custom 'nearly always permitted the copyholder of inheritance to surrender his holding to the use of another party for a term of years or for the term of the life of this second party', and these limited surrenders were convenient instruments for those wishing to lease out their lands. The fines paid on these limited surrenders were 'usually nominal', and during them the copyholder of inheritance reserved the remainder to himself and his heirs. ibid., p.41, 49–50; Clay, 'Landlords and estate management', p.334; Bettey, 'Land tenure', p.36; Campbell, *English Yeoman*, pp.129–30, 143–4.
21. Kerridge, *Agrarian Problems*, pp.48–53; C. J. Harrison, 'Elizabethan village surveys: a comment', *Agricultural History Review*, vol. 27 (1979), p.88; Hipkin, 'Penny rent', p.9.
22. Overton, *Agricultural Revolution*, p.35; A. Everitt, 'Farm Labourers', in Thirsk (ed.), *Agrarian History*, IV, p.401n.; Bowden, 'Agricultural prices', p.689; Hipkin, 'Tenant farming', pp.646, 672–3. Having drawn attention to Brenner's failure to consider 'the customary tenant as landlord', two of his early critics noted that 'subletting is largely ignored when surveys are analysed because evidence for it is so sparse and cannot be readily analysed statistically, though it is usually acknowledged that subletting may substantially alter the picture presented by the surveys'. P. Croot and D. Parker, 'Agrarian class structure and the development of capitalism', in Aston and Philpin (eds), *The Brenner Debate*, pp.81–2 and n.10. Kerridge himself was adamant that it is 'impossible to trace more than a fraction of the subtenancies and sublettings of demesne, socage and customary lands', Kerridge, *Agrarian Problems*, p.52.
23. Kerridge, *Agrarian Problems*, pp.49, 166–73; Hipkin, 'Penny rent', p.9; Chalklin, *Kent*, pp.58–9; Harrison, 'Elizabethan village surveys', pp.86–7.
24. Hipkin, 'Tenant farming', p.673: Idem, 'The structure of landownership and land occupation in the Romney Marsh region, 1646–1834', *Agricultural History Review* (forthcoming, 2003).
25. Harrison, 'Elizabethan village surveys', p.88 n.21; Glennie, 'In search of agrarian capitalism', pp.24–5.
26. One reason why manorial lords were willing to 'sell' lands for fines prior to the civil war was the lack of any other way to use land as security to raise long-term capital. By the late seventeenth century the mortgage had been developed to meet this demand.

27. Clay, *Economic Expansion*, p.89; Lambeth Palace Library, Mss 737, ff.16–18.
28. P. Bowden, 'Agricultural prices, farm profits, and rents', in J. Thirsk (ed.), The *Agrarian History of England and Wales, Vol. IV, 1500–1640* (Cambridge, 1967), pp.593–695; Overton, *Agricultural Revolution*, pp.16–22; Clay, *Economic Expansion*, pp.92–101.
29. ibid., pp.93–4; Hipkin, 'Penny rent', p.9.
30. For some recent discussion of the historiography of post-Restoration trends see Allen, *Enclosure and the Yeoman*, pp.78–104. After 1692 small owners also suffered from the heavy burden of the land tax.
31. Campbell, *English Yeoman*, p.119; Bettey, 'Land tenure', p.36; Clay, 'Landlords and estate management', p.334.
32. Such farming survived into the nineteenth century, indeed in the Romney Marsh region there was something of a *revival* of subsistence farming during the Napoleonic wars. Hipkin, 'Land ownership and land occupation', (forthcoming); M. Reed, 'The peasantry of nineteenth-century England: a neglected class', *History Workshop*, vol. 18 (1984), *passim*.
33. Wordie's estimates are not universally accepted, but he suggests that about 45 per cent of the land was enclosed by 1500, 2 per cent was enclosed during the sixteenth century, 24 per cent during the seventeenth century, 13% during the eighteenth century and 11 per cent in the nineteenth century. J. R. Wordie, 'The chronology of English enclosure, 1500–1914', *Economic History Review*, vol.36 (1983), pp.483–505. The most detailed general treatment of enclosure is J.A. Yelling, *Common Field and Enclosure in England, 1450–1850* (London, 1977).
34. Hipkin, 'Penny rent', pp.16–17.
35. B. Sharp, *In Contempt of All Authority: rural artisans and riot in the west of England, 1586–1660* (Berkeley, 1980), pp.5–6, 126–55, 257–63; K. Lindley, *Fenland Riots and the English Revolution* (London, 1982), pp.255–7; C. Holmes, 'Drainers and fenmen: the problem of popular political consciousness in the seventeenth century', in A. Fletcher and J. Stevenson (eds), *Order and Disorder in Early Modern England* (Cambridge, 1985), pp.179–83, 185.
36. Hipkin, 'Penny rent', pp.15–16, 20–1: *Idem*, 'The impact of marshland drainage on Rye harbour', in J. Eddison (ed.), *Romney Marsh: the debatable ground* (Oxford, 1995), pp.138–47; Overton, *Agricultural Revolution*, pp.157–8.
37. Hipkin, 'Penny rent', pp.22–3, 27–9. E.P. Thompson, *Customs in Common*, (Harmondsworth, 1993) pp.132–43, has traced in some detail the 're-ification of usages into properties which could be rented, sold or willed', that took place 'from the time of Coke to that of Blackstone'. As this 'hardening and concretion of the notion of property' progressed, '"attaching Rights to place, or in other words to inanimate matter, instead of to the person independently of place"' as Tom Paine put it, so the law disallowed the usages of the many, and the legitimacy of such loose, socially inclusive notions of custom as had sustained the usages of the many. But Thompson I think greatly underestimates just how concrete notions of rights as property were *before* Coke's time, and how deeply they had permeated thinking at all levels of society. When copyholders

collectively asserted right of common based on manorial custom they advanced often elaborately contractual claims to ownership, sometimes in severely exclusive terms.
38. S. Hindle, 'Persuasion and protest in the Caddington Common enclosure dispute 1635–1639', *Past and Present,* vol.158 (1998), pp.72–3, 75: Chalklin, *Kent,* pp.21–2; Thompson, *Customs,* p.130.
39. People did however, have a sense of belonging to broad groups defined by the massive inequalities of wealth that were the *net result* of the structure of property relations. 'Poor men' knew themselves and sometimes expressed themselves as such, though their sense of belonging was rarely articulated in sustained, organised representative institutions capable of giving this consciousness a cutting political edge. The 'rich and powerful' had no shortage of organised and institutionalised opportunities to express their sense of group identity. In 1604, the newly created 'freemen' of the Liberty of Romney Marsh declared themselves 'the chiefest, substantialist, most sufficient, discreetest and richest inhabitants of the commonalty'. S. Hipkin, 'The worlds of Daniel Langdon; public office and private enterprise in the Romney Marsh region in the early-eighteenth century', in A. Long, S. Hipkin and H. Clarke (eds), *Romney Marsh: coastal and landscape change through the ages,* (Oxford, 2002), p.183.
40. R.B. Manning, *Village Revolts: social protest and popular disturbances in England, 1509–1640* (Oxford, 1988) provides a descriptive inventory of many resource allocation disputes.
41. Principally inspired, of course, by the work of E.P. Thompson. For a useful discussion of the historiography see A. Wood, *The Politics of Social Conflict: the Peak country, 1520–1770* (Cambridge, 1999), pp.10–18.

A Tribute
Rodney Hilton 1916–2002

With the death of Rodney Hilton in June 2002 our journal has lost one of its most distinguished advisers and the country one of its greatest medieval historians. Arguably, Hilton did for medieval peasants what E.P. Thompson did for workers and artisans by rescuing them from the 'enormous condescension of posterity'. His achievement in illuminating the active part played by the peasantry themselves in the processes which ultimately led to the dissolution of feudalism was a remarkable one, combining meticulous research, careful judgements and a preoccupation with the wider picture. Hilton married an insistence on the capacity of the peasantry for struggle against exploitation with a subtle understanding of what such struggle might or might not achieve. His extended but brilliantly succinct pamphlet on the *Decline of Serfdom in Medieval England*, brought together the fruits of his early researches and reflections; it remains an indispensable introduction to the subject, providing a disciplined and lucid explanation of what he called the 'equivocal end' of English serfdom.[1] Hilton subsequently placed the struggles of the English peasantry in a European context in *Bond Men Made Free*—another absolutely essential study for those wishing to understand the nature and evolution of medieval peasant movements as well as the society which produced them.[2]

Rodney Hilton played a prominent part in the decision of the Historians' Group of the CPGB, of which he was chairman, to launch the journal *Past & Present* in 1952, himself contributing an article on the emergence of capitalism to its very first issue.[3] This appeared in the context of the famous debate generated by Paul Sweezy and Maurice Dobb on the 'Transition From Feudalism to Capitalism'. Over twenty years later, Hilton returned to this theme, editing an expanded updated collection of the original essays to which he contributed himself.[4] A decade later *Past & Present* appropriately enough provided the vehicle for the resumption of discussion about the genesis of capitalism drawing in a variety of specialists in European history and commanding widespread interest. Hilton's own contribution to this debate was entitled 'A Crisis of Feudalism' and served to underline the effectiveness with which he brought the Marxist concept of a mode of production to bear on empirical data.[5] Although trenchant in his dislike of abstract theorising and of theorists who did no real history Hilton was always comfortable when deploying ideas derived from classical Marxism or grappling with elusive terms like 'feudalism' or 'the peasant economy'. According to his *Guardian* obituarist Christopher Dyer, the essays based on Hilton's Ford lectures which he delivered in 1973 contain 'the most satisfying discussion of the term "peasant" found in any recent historical writing'.[6]

The consistency of Hilton's historical outlook went hand-in-hand with an abiding political and social commitment. Although he left the Communist Party as a result of the crises of 1956 he was to rejoin in the 1980s and became an honorary vice-president of the Socialist History Society. Any suggestion that political commitment and academic rigour were incompatible was entirely foreign to Hilton, a position which may be seen to be justified by a body of writings which remain as influential as they are stimulating.

David Parker is on the Editorial Board of Socialist History

Notes

1. Rodney Hilton, *The Decline of Serfdom in Medieval England* (London, 1969).
2. Rodney Hilton, *Bond Men Made Free. Medieval peasant movements and the English rising of 1381* (London, 1973).
3. Rodney Hilton, 'Capitalism—What's In a Name', *Past & Present*, vol.1 (1952), pp.32–43.
4. Rodney Hilton, 'The Transition From Feudalism to Capitalism' (London, 1976).
5. Rodney Hilton, 'A Crisis of Feudalism', *Past & Present*, vol.80 (1978), pp.3–19 reprinted in T.H. Aston and C.H.E. Philpin (eds), *The Brenner Debate* (Cambridge, 1985), pp.119–37.
6. Christopher Dyer in the *Guardian*, 10 June 2002. The lectures were published as *The English Peasantry in the Later Middle Ages* (Oxford, 1975).

Reviews

Books to be remembered (6)

Alan Winnington, *Breakfast with Mao. Memoirs of a Foreign Correspondent*, London, 1986.

This is a lively and very readable book, of both general and historical interest. The author was present at certain historical events when no other Western journalist was present, and it remains a record which is significant. Alan Winnington was born into a lower middle class family whose father had lifted them up from an average working class existence. Alan went to an elementary school where flogging and caning were common practices, and then to a small public school whose headmaster was also a persistent flogger. He was born just before the First World War. His life in the 1930s was a mixture of low grade employment, and unemployment. He became a quite active communist and was refused military service during the Second World War, on political grounds. He joined the staff of the *Daily Worker*, and in 1948 was sent to China at the request of the Chinese Communist Party, who wanted an experienced journalist for their information department. These were historic years for China. The Kuomintang was collapsing and the communists were planning to take over Beijing and the government of the whole country. Winnington became on friendly terms with leading communists and he was among the first to enter peacefully the beautiful old city, years later to be so disgracefully vandalised.

In June 1950 he was the guest at an informal supper with Mao Zedong, Zhou Enlai, Chu De (the leading military commander) and other personalities. Their discussion was concerned with the many problems of a now peaceful country, such as land reform and industrialisation; it was Mao who insisted that they must reduce the size of their armed forces.

Five days later the Korean war began, and demobilisation was with regret postponed. Winnington found himself almost immediately in North Korea as the correspondent of the *Daily Worker* and the Chinese agency. The Korean war was grossly misrepresented in the British press, and information to the world was largely dominated by the American military and a mostly client American press. For months Winnington was the only western journalist in North Korea and it was later that he was joined by Wilfred Burchett, an Australian representing the Paris *Ce Soir*.

When the front was finally stabilised along the 38th Parallel, and peace negotiations were raggedly proceeded with, Winnington became steadily more important for accurate accounts of the negotiations. The American military proved incapable of presenting a truthful resume of what was being considered, and increasingly the serious journalists on the south Korean front were willing to accept Winnington's version, since he had seen daily the relevant documents. The American military were not amused.

There were, of course, units of the British army in Korea. It was, theoretically, an operation sanctioned by the United Nations, and agreed largely because of the temporary absence of the Soviet Union from the UN Council. About four and a half thousand British troops were in action: 749 were killed, a further 159 listed as missing, 2556 were wounded and 978 taken prisoner. The British government, it always should be remembered, did nothing for these prisoners and, as in all matters, remained subservient to the Americans. Winnington hesitated for several months before he began visiting the prisoners of war camps. The British Communist Party was on the whole against contact, on the grounds that both Winnington and the *Daily Worker* would be liable to legal charges of consorting with the enemy. There were, however, increasing pressures upon Winnington, not least from the British prisoners' committees which were always established by the soldiers themselves. Here are his own words:

> In the short time that my paper would spare me from the truce talks there was plenty to do (in the British prison camps, that is). Taking mail; although there was official mail exchange, the POWs did not trust it but preferred me to send it via Tokyo or Beijing. There were constant demands to speak at camp meetings. I had chances to arrange marriages by proxy so that girl friends at home could draw some pay. One day I got some cine stock to feed into my 35mm camera and took photographs of all five hundred or so Britons in No 5 camp to send to their next of kin. On a brief visit to Beijing I bought skates, footballs and playing cards of which they never had enough. As a group they were irrepressible and full of fun. I ate with them, went skating on the river with them and smoked my first marijuana with them. It grew wild on the nearby hills…(p.164)

When the war was over Winnington was denounced as a collaborator and guilty of helping to 'brainwash' British prisoners, and his passport was taken away; to be returned nearly twenty years later. No one who had been a prisoner ever substantiated these accusations. The contrary. Winnington always maintained relations with some of the ex-prisoners and when his passport was returned, he continued with personal contacts.

One interesting contrast between the Americans and the British: the former, of course, had many more in their army and larger numbers of prisoners, but the death rate among all Americans was astonishingly high. There was, it should be noted, no brutality towards any of the prisoners by either Chinese or Koreans. Life was never easy, but the absence of deliberate cruelty has been accepted. Yet American morale was appalling, and of those made prisoner with the same kind of regime as the British about one-third engaged in some kind of collaboration; and of the total of 7,190 prisoners, some 2,730 died (or about 38 per cent). These differences, Winnington suggests, came out of the kind of society the two nations lived in, with the British tradition of solidarity and trade unionism helping to explain these extraordinary statistics.

One large unresolved question is still a matter of historical controversy, and until the Americans are prepared to release all the relevant documentation we shall not know the complete story. The accusation that America had experimented with biological weapons became so powerful that an international commission was brought together to explore the problem in Korea. Joseph Needham, one of our great names in science in the twentieth century, was a member and for the rest of his life he continued to believe that the commission's findings—of this infamous American practice—were never in doubt. In a letter to the Dean of Canterbury a decade or so after the commission's visit he wrote that 'the American side did try experiments with bacteriological warfare, using insect vectors and means broadly of that kind'.

When the war finally ended Winnington returned to Beijing. He loved China, but life was becoming more difficult with the signs of the Great Leap Forward beginning to uncover its absurdities. He left China at the end of the 1950s, and without a British passport spent nearly two decades in Berlin during which time he wrote three novels and six crime stories. He visited Britain only occasionally, married a German woman, and died in November 1983, having nearly completed this present volume: 'a brilliantly readable book' wrote Neal Ascherson in his introductory Foreword. And a book of the life of a remarkable personality.

Note

The literature on the Korean war is voluminous. At the time there was a pamphlet by Sir John Pratt, *Korea. The Lie that Led to War* (1952) which is still worth reading. Pratt worked for many years at the Foreign Office and was a specialist on Far Eastern affairs. There is a major work of two massive volumes by Bruce Cumings who does not accept the usual American argument that the war was begun by an invasion of South Korea by the North. The Cold War International Project published a study of the Russian archives by Kathryn Weathersby in November 1993; but let me say again that the literature is large and by no means unfinished.

John Saville is professor emeritus at the University of Hull and president of the Oral History Society.

Summer of 1972

Ralph Darlington and Dave Lyddon, *Glorious Summer. Class Struggle in Britain, 1972* (Bookmarks, London, Chicago and Sydney, 2001) ISBN 1 898876 68 1, xii+304pp., £13.99pbk.

As the authors point out in their introduction, 'this book is the first systematic attempt to bring together and analyse the major industrial movement of 1972'. In their conclusion, they refer to it as 'a guidebook of militant working class struggle'. It begins with a look at the industrial and political background to the events of 1972, and then devotes a chapter each to the national pit strike, the railway work-to-rule, the engineering sit-ins in Greater Manchester, the dockers and the Industrial Relations Act, and the building industry strike, concluding with a look at what the authors consider to be the lessons of all the struggles of that year. The account is drawn mainly from newspapers and political weeklies, but also from trade union and employers' records where possible. There is a useful chronology of the events, a note-apparatus and lengthy list of sources, an index and some photographs. To cover the momentous events of that year in one book and do them justice is quite an achievement. On the whole, in my opinion, the authors have done so.

Darlington and Lyddon pay tribute to individual members of Britain's Communist Party (CPGB) and groupings of them, who played a key role in the disputes covered, often being the leading figures at the rank-and-file level, sometimes at district or national level, of the union(s) concerned. However, a theme running through the book is the CPGB's perceived line of prioritising the election of left-wing officials into full-time union posts over encouraging a radical shop stewards' movement at the rank-and-file level. Darlington and Lyddon trace this back to the establishment of the Anglo-Russian Trade Union Unity Committee [ARC] in 1924 (p.28), which gave a 'false radical credibility' to the left-wingers on the TUC General Council and was used to discourage independent rank-and-file initiatives during the 1926 General Strike. From then on, the authors claim, loyalty to Moscow, to whatever Stalin wished, determined the CPGB's trade union policy.

An enormous debate could, indeed should, take place around this theme. It is, of course, Trotsky's argument put in its crudest way. The TUC did bottle out, the lefts on the General Council did fail, and the rank-and-file were unprepared—true. But Trotsky exaggerated the impact of all this for his own factional ends, and since then his followers have uncritically repeated it ad nauseam. Darlington and Lyddon would profit by reading the essay on it by Alexander Vatlin in *Die Komintern 1919–29* (Mainz, 1993), based on newly accessible archive materials. They focus purely on the negative result of the ARC, as did Trotsky himself, possibly unaware of the positive side. In fact, the creation of the ARC led to a massive revival of the movement for international trade union unity in Europe. It put the right wing on the defensive and resulted in unity committees being set up in almost all European countries. The Norwegian, Finnish and other union centres expressed the wish to adhere to the ARC. A similar outfit was set up in Scandinavia. The Soviet leadership let the right wing off the hook by giving up the campaign under the pressure of the sectarians. The ARC then became a political bloc between the two components but turned out to be useless when British imperialism acted in China and raided Soviet institutions in London, not to mention the question of the British General Strike and miners' struggle. The events of 1926 were the last gasp of the post-war struggles and not a new rising wave, thus revolution was not thwarted, neither was the CPGB wholly subservient to Moscow, as arguments over the 'new line' in 1929 show, nor was Stalin able to determine policy by himself.

In the background chapter the Upper Clyde Shipbuilders' (UCS) 'work-in' and its impact are described. It 'won considerable sympathy…from trade unionists across the country'. (p.22) I would say that it won solidarity and was met with enthusiasm all over Europe. I recall UCS representatives speaking to shipbuilders in Copenhagen. The closure of Saltley Gates by mass picketing during the pit strike, as portrayed in chapter 2, must have terrified the capitalist class elsewhere in Europe. *Arbejdsgiveren*, the organ of the Danish employers' organisation, had a photo of the 1,000 coppers marching away from the locked gates as pickets rejoiced, and commented: 'It must never happen here'. So the events of 1972 had an international dimension.

Following a failure to attain serious concessions from the employers, the engineering union (AUEW) leadership decided on a policy of plant bargaining, taking the view that a national strike would have been both difficult to organise, owing to lengthy procedural rules, and potentially risky, owing to unemployment and the depressed state of the industry. Manchester then became the centre of a quite unique struggle in which dozens of factories would be occupied by the workforce in various forms. The CPGB occupied leading positions in the AUEW structure and at the lay level. It had led the way in building up a broad left in the union, which had succeeded in getting Hugh Scanlon, a former communist and very capable left-winger, elected as AUEW president. The problems, the ins and outs, and the results of the struggle are presented here in some detail, but in spite of great gains being made in a number of cases on wages, hours, etc, the results overall were patchy, owing to the plant bargaining strategy. Scanlon wanted the strongest organised factories to spearhead the fight, but this did not happen. Quoting John Tocher, at that time the AUEW's divisional organiser and a CPGB member, Darlington and Lyddon portray a sense of disillusionment and a setback from which the broad left was never to recover because huge sacrifices had brought little to some of those involved. Yet they also quote, correctly in my view, another author who pointed out the groundbreaking nature of the sit-ins, the fact that they were offensive not defensive and represented an 'Olympian leap in consciousness'. (p.120) The sit-ins were 'a missed opportunity for the left', and it can be put down to the authors' hobby-horse, the focus of the leading stewards 'on union structures (rather) than on shopfloor organisation' (p.134). Not just the district officials but the left-wing AUEW leaders ought to have been challenged, and the bulletin issued during the dispute by the International Socialists (forerunner of the SWP, to which the authors belong) does make a few critical points though is otherwise loyal. But the problem with this view is that Scanlon, Tocher, *et al.* were far ahead of most AUEW members, and in any case the strategy advanced by Scanlon was not being followed. One has to ask whether the consciousness existed that could have produced any other outcome.

The chapter on the dockers and the Industrial Relations Act (written with Fred Lindop) deals with the unofficial picketing which attempted to stop containerisation taking work outside of the docks, and with how the Heath government's anti-union legislation was used: in particular, how political intervention led to changed judgements. For example, the National Industrial Relations Court (NIRC), set up under the 1971 act, decided at first that the TGWU was responsible for the actions of its shop stewards when Liverpool dockers blacked a transport firm, fined the union for contempt for not stopping the action, and fined it again three weeks later. The same judgement was made in relation to a case in Hull. But in London the NIRC named the shop stewards' committee and three named dockers rather than the relevant unions, the TGWU and NASD (National Association of Stevedores and Dockers). The following day, the Court of Appeal, in the shape of Lord Denning, upheld the TGWU's case against the NIRC and cancelled the earlier fines. Denning, an arch-reactionary hostile to trade unionism, was defending the law as such and endeavouring to maintain its appearance of impartiality. However, in holding individuals responsible he 'effectively destroyed the basis of government strategy'. (p.156)

Following this another firm went to the NIRC to get an order to stop picketing by London dockers; seven were named, though none ever appeared before it. After a couple of weeks the firm returned to the NIRC because the dockers had ignored the order, and the result was an arrest warrant for five of the dockers. The five were put in Pentonville prison and that became the focus for the protest movement. Unofficial strikes began to spread, and on 26 July 'after five days of escalating unofficial strike action, the TUC General Council voted for a one-day national stoppage'. (p.169) On the same day the Law Lords overturned the Court of Appeal's ruling and insisted that the TGWU was responsible for the actions of its shop stewards, and so the five dockers were released, though they had been gaoled for contempt of the NIRC, not for the their original actions. The ruling class had got itself off the hook by a legal manoeuvre, though 'most of the press (saw the release of the five as) a serious defeat for both the government and the rule of law'. (p.174) Denning regarded the Industrial Relations Act as having 'been shattered' and the NIRC as having been shown 'to be powerless' (p.175). An enormous working-class victory had been won, although the dockers lost the battle against containerisation as the TGWU did not oppose it. One inaccuracy in this account is the claim that the NASD had a 'significant membership' in Liverpool (p.143) at this time. As far as I can recall, it had shrunk to a rump by then.

The chapter on the building strike refers to it as a 'great revolt', very aptly in my opinion, describing how the rank and file 'escalated the dispute into an all-out strike involving mass and flying pickets in which many Communist Party members were prominent at local level'. (p.179) The building unions were very weak by this time due to the growth of 'lumpers' who were not employed directly but subcontracted. The backbone of the strike was the Building Workers' Charter group, established in 1970 on the initiative of the CPGB activists. Its demands included £35 for 35 hours, abolition of the lump, one union for the industry, and greater union democracy. The organ of the movement was selling 10,000 per issue in its first year. The charter won the support of UCATT, an amalgamation of the main craft unions, for a national claim of £30 for 35 hours in December 1971. In late June strikes began at selected sites to hit the big firms. An attempt at a sell-out was halted and by mid-August an all-out strike was underway. Lou Lewis, a leading CPGB activist in London is quoted: after a 'big meeting in the Conway Hall…I laid out the Joint Sites Committee strategy, all-out with no strike pay. And from that moment on the leadership lost any grip of it…I was the co-ordinator in London…It was like a military operation' (p.194). Teams of pickets were sent out to every job, and Ricky Tomlinson (the actor), then a picketing co-ordinator on the Chester and North Wales Action Committee, talks of how 'we put the rest of the country to shame because we had a 99 percent success rate. No one worked'. Pickets were sent all over to close every job down. Hence, 'the leadership of the trade union movement, UCATT and the T&G, became panicky, because we'd actually taken the reins from them, we were actually calling the shots'. (p.197)

The dispute was ended in mid-September by UCATT's sell-out. Craftsmen got a 30 per cent rise on basic pay, 'the largest…ever won in the industry', but it was widely felt by those who were active during the strike that a couple more weeks would have led to a total victory. Instead the lump returned with a vengeance, along with the victimisation of activists. I feel that the criticism of the role of the CPGB is well founded here. For example, the Building Workers' Charter paper did not appear during the thirteen weeks of the strike. Perhaps none of the militants had the time, but the authors claim that 'some CP members were opposed to the Charter initiative and were more interested in obtaining official posts within the unions or establishing close relationships with existing left-wing full-time officials…The latter was closer to official CP industrial policy as a whole and…it was to increasingly determine Charter policies after the strike' (p.200). The *Morning Star* even made space for a half-page article by the right-wing UCATT boss and sell-out merchant George Smith.

The ruling-class backlash resulted in a series of trials for 'intimidation' against North Wales pickets in Mold during the summer of 1973; all were found not guilty. A further 24 pickets were then tried in Shrewsbury, the scene of the alleged offences, but in order to secure convictions, six were charged with other offences and 'conspiracy to intimidate' being the means. John McKinsie Jones, Ricky Tomlinson and Des Warren ended up with nine-month, two-year and three-year gaol sentences respectively. The employers' blacklist saw to it that the militants were gradually rooted out of the industry and

UCATT was severely weakened. Though not covered in this book, the CPGB's attitude to the Shrewsbury case, the allegations of malpractices and being hand-in-hand with the bosses on the part of some UCATT officials, including the odd Communist Party member and others it helped into office, could be considered when discussing official CP policy towards UCATT.

The last chapter sums up what the authors see as the lessons of the 1972 struggles. Some of the points raised are valid, particularly those concerning the CP's attitude to trade union officialdom as opposed to rank-and-file movements. But such movements come and go, based as they are around limited demands, whereas trade union officialdom is a permanent feature: therefore both have to be taken into account by class-war protagonists. Trotskyism took from the Comintern many of its negative features, among them the tendency to focus on leadership, and denounce it for betrayal if it wasn't thought of as doing its duty, at the expense of the consciousness existing among the 'led', who were perhaps disinclined to go as far as the communists wished. That tendency is present in this book, but on the whole it is an excellent analysis of the events of 1972.

> *Mike Jones writes and translates on the history of Marxism. He is a former member of the CPGB and SWP who in 1972 was a member of the International Socialists, living and working in Denmark*

Deep in the comintern archives

Andrew Thorpe, *The British Communist Party and Moscow 1920–43* (Manchester University Press, Manchester, 2000) ISBN 0 7190 5312 9, xii+308pp., £45.

With this book Andrew Thorpe has performed a great service to historians of British communism. As he notes in his introduction, the Comintern archives now accessible in Moscow provide a wealth of material for the first two decades of the party's history, and internationally there has been an explosion of new scholarship focusing on relations between the Comintern's national sections and Moscow. On the other hand, work on the archives is a pretty daunting enterprise. Their bulk, complexity and location means that research is time-consuming, expensive and not easily carried out in conjunction with work on other relevant materials. Key documents relating to the CPGB are not always available in English, with German, Russian and sometimes French being the main other languages used. Assumed identities and the frequently opaque allusions in correspondence between London and Moscow also have to be negotiated. Not least, there are well in excess of a thousand files of possible relevance for the CPGB, and most have to be consulted without the advantage of detailed finding aids.

To set out to produce a dense empirical narrative from these materials is thus a formidable undertaking. Coming to the task as a highly regarded historian of the Labour Party, Thorpe brings to it two invaluable assets. One is that he has come to the subject relatively fresh, without any particular historiographical axe to grind, and hence without the temptation simply to quarry the archives simply for the confirmation of existing views. The other is a readiness to put in what looks like years of work into making sense of the materials he has consulted. Given the current institutional pressures for a quick and repetitive turnover of publications, this is a virtue in itself. Anybody who has looked at the same archives can only be impressed by the tremendous skill with which he has a provided a lucid, fair and reliable representation of what they contain. His work is slightly reminiscent of the writings on the Comintern of E. H. Carr, and he bears comparison with Carr in his ability to summarise and make sense of highly involved political exchanges, in which what was not said was often as important as what was. Given the relative inaccessibility of these archives, his book provides an invaluable resource for those who may disagree with its interpretative framework as well as those who share it.

As observations rather than criticisms, three particular features of the approach he has taken may be noted. One is its setting very much within the context of the 'centre-periphery' debate concerning the extent and character of the Comintern's controls over its national sections. Though this issue dominated the historiography of the 1990s, and a contribution of this scale from a British perspective was very much in order, internationally there are signs that the debate is now moving on. Probably nobody who is not politically committed to doing so any longer holds to the 'strong' view of Moscow control, which in the CPGB's case—like the 'strong' view of the party's autonomy—is simply too easily disproven on the basis of the evidence now available. Hence, to steer a middle course between these polarities, as Thorpe proposes in his introduction, is, or should be, in many ways uncontroversial. Perhaps because almost nobody in Britain has argued that the Comintern 'made no real difference' to the communists' daily work (p.4), Thorpe's narrative stance does tend to be that of qualifying and contesting the 'strong' view of Moscow control, and the early signs are that this is provoking responses a good deal less sophisticated than his own. Even so, the future of communist history does not lie in this direction.

Perhaps a more significant point is that Thorpe's provision of a 'thick' chronological narrative does allow one or two issues to slip through the net.

What he provides is a complex story, in which issues of policy, communications, funding and personnel are very adeptly linked with developments in communist politics both in Britain and Russia. On the other hand, even in the context of a basically institutional study, fuller consideration might have been given to issues like cadre formation, including the role of the Lenin School, and the functioning of the party's front organisations. There might also have been more space for a comparative evaluation of the CPGB's relations with the Comintern over time. Though Thorpe's emphasis on the continuous interplay between centre and periphery is obviously justified, arguably he gives too even an impression of this relationship, so that the extent to which the balance between autonomy and control shifted during the life of the Comintern is not fully brought out. This is particularly an issue with regard to the Third Period. Though clearly the Comintern's domination of its British section was never absolute, the extent to which its interventions were more systematic and more intrusive during this period than both before and afterwards does not seem to me sufficiently conveyed. On comparative criteria, rather than those of the cruder 'Cold War' accounts which Thorpe rightly dismisses, it still seems hard to think of the examples in British history when a political party was more responsive to external stimuli than the CPGB during Class Against Class.

Finally, given the scale of the task he has undertaken, it is inevitable that what Thorpe has provided us with is very much the view from the Moscow archives. He has made excellent use of a selection of other materials, primarily archival, and of what secondary literature there is. Even so, it is possible that regarding a number of key events and personalities a broader context and range of sources might suggest slightly different interpretations to those he advances. For example, the functionaries responsible for the party's formal communications might loom larger than they perhaps ought to: a 'factional' meeting in 1922 is described as chiefly comprising 'second-rank figures', although even from the perspective of his Moscow connections it not clear that this is an adequate description of somebody like W.N. Ewer, the *Daily Herald*'s foreign editor and one of the most influential disseminators of communist opinion in this period. Similarly, though I am sure it is right that Palme Dutt has been accorded too central a role by historians (including this one) reliant on his papers, there are still major issues to be explained concerning Dutt's links with the Comintern's Anglo-American secretariat and clandestine centre in Brussels; and the way in which during twelve years not resident in Britain, he was one of only four communists to remain continuously on the CPGB's central committee! There is also the unexplained anomaly of his control over the *Labour*

Monthly, and the opportunity this gave him for a regular public exposition of the party line that was widely regarded as authoritative without always avoiding questions of internal party controversy. In a sense, that only confirms Thorpe's important argument that the lines of command and communication were very often more fragmented than we tended to believe prior to the opening of the archives.

There are therefore many other angles on the CPGB's history still to be explored, and for these Thorpe offers an indispensable point of reference. On the whole, his book provides a measured, insightful and thoroughly researched account of what remains the most controversial aspect of the party's history.

Kevin Morgan has written widely on communist party history

A twentieth-century party

Duncan Tanner, Pat Thane and Nick Tiratsoo (eds), *Labour's First Century* (Cambridge University Press, Cambridge, 2000) ISBN 0 52165 184 0, 428pp., £30.

The origins of the Labour Party date back to 1900 with the formation of the Labour Representation Committee (LRC), an organisation set up by the trade unions who were struggling against anti-union laws. This book examines the party's role throughout the twentieth century, outlining both its strengths and its weaknesses, the controversies which took place both within and without and its prospects for the future. It is not a chronological history but twelve separate essays in which the writers concentrate on special subjects.

Jose Harris, writing on 'Labour's political and social thought', shows how the founders of the LRC were in no doubt that many aspects of the constitutional arrangements that then existed were unfairly stacked against them; early party conferences supported reforms, such as abolition of the House of Lords and universal suffrage. The industrial conflicts during the First World War, together with the enlargement of state power after 1919, reawakened suspicions that the state was not an impartial mediator of differing interests, but a 'sinister conglomerate of upper-class power'. 'Clause 4', inserted into Labour's constitution in 1918 and advocating 'common ownership of the means of production, distribution and exchange', was to remain in its constitution until 1995.

Jim Tomlinson explores the development of Labour's ideas, and what these have achieved in practice. He suggests that twentieth century British economic policy can be summarised as 'a process of the rise, consolidation, and eventual weakening of national government economic management'. Labour has been a major contributor to this process, but its approach has been 'fundamentally affected by the need for modernisation'.

In 'Labour and welfare', Pat Thane quotes Ramsay MacDonald speaking in 1907 of the poverty-stricken lives of the unemployed and their families and emphasising the duty of the state to take action, not just relieve suffering. His words were followed by a series of bills demanding the right to work or full maintenance, all of which were defeated. Thane describes the 'Poor Law' and how it worked. However, in 1924, when MacDonald became prime minister in a minority government, little was done to improve welfare except in the case of the famous Housing Act, initiated by John Wheatley of Glasgow, under which subsidies for council house building were much increased, and former restrictions on such building abolished.

Throughout the 1920s, Labour played an increasing role in local government, but the big changes came in 1945. During this period, with Attlee as prime minister, the National Insurance Act was introduced, under which, in return for contributions, working people were entitled to pensions and other benefits, such as Unemployment Benefit. These years also saw the introduction of the National Health Service.

In 1964–70, under the Wilson government, NHS prescription charges were abolished and pensions increased, while during the 1970s—again under Wilson and later James Callaghan—further important steps were taken, including the Child Benefit Act introduced by Barbara Castle in 1975.

In his essay on 'Labour and international affairs', Stephen Howe describes the early debates and disputes within the party between the 'anti-colonialists' and those who wanted to retain the British Empire; and how, under the Attlee government, some of the major colonies—for example India, Pakistan, Sri Lanka and Burma—were at last granted freedom. Other issues of continual dispute have been the party's attitudes to war, and more recently Britain's commitment to nuclear weapons.

Miles Taylor shows how, from its beginning, the party was arguing for radical reforms, how its manifesto 'Labour and the New Social Order', among other things, not only committed the party to abolition of the House of Lords but also to separate assemblies for Scotland, Wales and England, and the transfer of responsibilities for retailing, public utilities and house building from central to local government.

Within the party there were continuing debates about the voting system with arguments both for and against the replacement of 'first-past-the-post' with proportional representation. Little was done to change the constitution until the arrival of the Blair government in 1997, under which separate assemblies have been granted to Scotland and Wales, while a system of proportional representation has been introduced for the elections to the European Parliament, and major reforms to the House of Lords are in progress.

Martin Francis explores the contribution made by women to the Labour Party's activities. The Women's Labour League came into existence in 1906 with a membership remaining at about 5000 until 1918, when it was replaced by 'women's sections' affiliated to local parties. This, and the extension of parliamentary suffrage to most women over 30, resulted in a massive surge of women joining the party. By 1922 they had reached 100,000 and the average female membership during the inter-war years was over a quarter of a million, which accounted for at least half the number of individual members.

At the same time, an increasing number of women were elected as local councillors; for instance, a quarter of those who won seats on the London County Council in 1931 were women. Francis outlines the major campaigns in which Labour women were involved, including workplace rights and the need for equal pay and conditions. While the number of female MPs was always much bigger than in the other parties, it remained very small—nine in 1929, 21 in 1945, 19 in 1966, 18 in October 1974. The first female cabinet member, Margaret Bondfield, was appointed by Ramsay MacDonald in 1929, but Ellen Wilkinson was the only woman in Attlee's cabinet in 1945. During the Wilson governments of 1964–70 and 1974–76 three women served in his cabinets—Barbara Castle, Judith Hart and Shirley Williams. However, the 'all-women' shortlists, introduced by the party in 1993, have caused much controversy.

Alan Reid suggests that at the end of the century, unions are playing a much less positive role in the Labour Party's affairs than would have been thought possible at any earlier point in its history. He describes how the Labour Party emerged as a result of trade union actions to secure more favourable legislation from the Liberal government which had held office before the First World War; the enormous expansion of union membership during that war; and how, from 1918 onwards, they participated in the policy-making of the newly formed Labour Party.

He tells how the unions raised money in support of the party both from individual membership subscriptions via the 'political levy' and the setting up of political funds; and the legal obstacles with which they were faced: for example, the 1927 Trades Disputes Act which, among other things, prohibited civil service unions from setting up political funds. It was not to be repealed until 1945 under the Attlee government.

In the Labour Party's earliest years, the bulk of Labour MPs were nominated by trade unions, and even after the growth of constituency parties, union-sponsored MPs remained very numerous; nine of them were in the Attlee cabinet. However, pressure on local constituency parties to adopt union-sponsored MPs caused some controversy and, as part of the 'modernisation' programme, union sponsorship was abolished in 1996.

What is known about the Labour Party's membership figures throughout these years is listed in an appendix to this book. The membership consisted of individual members, trade union members who paid their subscriptions via the political levy, and members of affiliated socialist and cooperative societies. In 1929, it numbered 2.3 million, of which 223,000 were individual members and just over 2 million trade union members. By 1947 the total was over 5 million; by 1952 it had reached 6 million, of which 1 million were individual members and 5 million trade unionists. The highest number recorded was in 1979 at 7.2 million, of which 6 million were from the trade unions, though the individual membership had fallen back to 666,000.

Duncan Tanner, writing on 'Labour and its membership', points out that the party has always relied on committed volunteers and activists to maintain its organisation. Its structure gave some power to activists at local level and through party conferences. But he points out that the attitudes of these activists and their views have often received much media attention: differences between members and leaders have always been highlighted. As a result, party leaders have often sought to direct the views of party members in the interests of electoral success and to limit their contribution to policy-making and policy debates.

In an essay on 'Labour and the electorate', Nick Tiratsoo points out that of the twenty-one general elections held between 1918 and 1992, only two yielded emphatic triumphs for Labour, while only once did the party come near to gaining 50 per cent of the votes cast. He describes how the party got 2.2 million votes in 1918, over 4 million in 1922 and 1923, and then reached 5.5 million in 1924—about one-third of the total, but enough to form a minority government. In 1929 Labour got 8.4 million votes—37 per cent of those cast—288 Labour MPs were elected and once again agreed to a minority government under Ramsay MacDonald. However, the British economy was facing unprecedented difficulties, and, in 1931 MacDonald defected to form a 'National' Government together with the Conservatives. Labour appeared discredited, ending up with 6.6 million votes but only 52 MPs. A slow recovery took place during the 1930s, but it was not until the postwar election in 1945 that it achieved its first real victory. It received nearly 12 million votes—48 per cent of the total—and ended up with a majority of 146 seats.

The swing to Labour was repeated at local elections. By 1947, the party controlled 52 of the 83 most important cities. However, in the next parliamentary election in February 1950, though the Labour vote went up to over 13 million, this was only 46.1 per cent of the vote, and the party ended up with a paltry five-seat majority. Twenty months later, though its vote rose again to 13.9 million—48.8 per cent of the poll—it lost its majority. The Conservatives took over for the next 13 years until Labour secured a narrow victory in 1964 under the leadership of Harold Wilson and then a more substantial triumph in 1966 based on 13 million votes or 48 per cent of the total.

However, this was to be a final highwater mark. Labour suffered defeat at the 1970 election, its share of the poll having fallen to 43.1 per cent. It was reelected as a minority government in February 1974 having only 37.2 per cent of the poll, but at a subsequent election eight months later it won 39.5 per cent of the votes and got a majority in parliament of just three seats.

In 1979, the Conservatives under Margaret Thatcher regained power and were to win the subsequent three elections. During this time, Labour was plagued with internal divisions, including the breakaway Social Democratic Party, and saw its share of vote collapse to 27.6 per cent in 1983. The subsequent years saw a slow recovery; in the 1987 election it received 30.8 per cent of the poll; in 1992, 34.4 per cent. However, during the 1990s with the 'modernisation' programme starting under Blair's leadership, views began to change, and in 1997, Labour achieved a majority of 174 seats with 13.5 million votes; however, this was still only 43.2 per cent of the votes cast.

Other interesting essays include one by Stefan Berger on 'Labour in comparative perspective', in which he makes a very interesting analysis of the differences between the labour movement in Britain and those in other countries—particularly Europe. Jon Lawrence examines 'Labour and the myths it has lived by'. The book ends with an overview by Steven Fielding on 'New Labour and the past' contrasting many of the earlier beliefs with those of the present day.

This book is a valuable source of information for both historians and those in the movement who are planning for a better future.

Noreen Branson is an editorial adviser to Socialist History

A story of wasted talent

Kathleen Burk, *Troublemaker: The Life and History of A.J.P. Taylor* (Yale University Press, New Haven and London, 2000) ISBN 0 3000 08761 6, 512pp., £22.50.

When in 1975 Taylor published his biography of Lord Beaverbrook, creator of the Express newspaper group, *Private Eye* cruelly referred to him as 'the ex-historian'. Certainly his uncritical fawning on the ghost of the shady press baron did his own reputation no favours (he was nearly 70 at the time) but it was no simple lapse—rather an exaggerated expression of Taylor's essential approach to history and historical writing.

Taylor, who was born in 1906, was not a very admirable individual—though he was far from being wholly contemptible either. His life can be viewed as a story of wasted talent—not in the usual sense, for he was phenomenally productive and extremely successful both as a self-publicist and as a money-maker—but rather in comparison to the historian he might have been.

Certainly he was splendidly equipped to stand beside such historians as E.P. Thompson, Christopher Hill and Eric Hobsbawm in pioneering a historiographical revolution. Unremittingly industrious, superbly organised, at home in four languages, a brilliant communicator both orally and on paper, he might have done for his specialism of diplomatic history what others did for social and cultural history—but his approach remained resolutely traditional.

Although his parents were affluent people Taylor's background was a left-wing one. His father and mother formed a ménage à trois with Henry Sara, a communist militant, and his father was buried in early 1940 in a coffin draped with the red flag and hammer and sickle—this at a time when the USSR was exceptionally unpopular on account of the Nazi-Soviet pact and the Finnish war. Taylor in his youth argued in favour of the USSR and Marxism, was a lifelong member of the Labour Party, helped to found CND and always regarded himself as a left-winger—though he had peculiar ideas of what left-wing might mean.

The book's title is pertinent to its subject—he was constantly at odds. Becoming a member of the Oxbridge academic establishment he was never fully accepted and was denied the honours and recognition he craved. To some extent this was due to his accomplishments in popular journalism and broadcasting, which were looked down upon as vulgar, but he almost always fell out too with the broadcasting controllers and newspaper editors.

Although Kathleen Burk was Taylor's student and, on the whole, his admirer, she doesn't try to conceal the unpleasant aspects of his personality which, apart from his historiographical sins, included financial meanness, lack of understanding towards his children and extreme insensitivity towards the women in his life. He refused invitations to take up professorships in Edinburgh and Manchester because that would have separated him from his academic network in the South East, but was aggrieved and bitter that he failed to win one in London or Oxbridge.

Such matters are never irrelevant in judging an individual but they would have shrunk in perspective if he had been among the twentieth-century historians who transformed the writing and understanding of history—which he certainly had the potential to have been. Awareness that he had travelled up a historiographical dead end possibly explains some at least of his rancour, self-pity and persecution complex. In compensation perhaps for his missing achievement he delighted in creating academic scandals and promoting himself as an enfant terrible.

Two episodes in particular stand out in this respect, the first being his endorsement of the claim put about in the late 1950s that the Nazis had no role in the Reichstag fire and that it was solely the action of the unfortunate van der Lubbe. More notoriously in 1961 came *The Origins of the Second World War*, which caused a public as well as an academic storm with its argument that Hitler had no worked-out scheme of European conquest but grabbed the opportunities which presented themselves, that his foreign policy perspectives were in line with those of the 1920s—and earlier—and that appeasement was quite a reasonable response in the circumstances.

Not that every part of his thesis was nonsensical, by any means. The point that Hitler was not simply a demon king who had erupted onto the European stage had been stressed often enough before, especially by Marxists, but had been largely ignored in the Cold War apologetics which found it convenient to portray him in this mode so as to validate a rearmed West Germany. Taylor, however, broke elementary historiographical rules by citing only evidence which suited his standpoint and ignoring or dismissing any which did not.

In addition Taylor ignored the significance of the social and political linkage of the Nazi rulers and the traditional establishment forces which had manoeuvred them into power, and he absurdly underplayed the dynamically aggressive character of the regime. In a review written at the time, Elizabeth Wiskemann remarked that she was surprised not to discover that the USSR had attacked Germany in 1941. (Indeed, some German historians of the revisionist school have lately argued just that.)

Burk tries bravely to defend the significance of *The Origins*, contending that whatever its shortcomings it has permanently altered the way in which the war's origins are viewed; but her arguments are not very convincing and they are even less so in relation to Taylor's volume in the *Oxford History of England* series, which is in fact one of the worst volumes in the series; superficial, rankly opinionated, and in which Taylor both displays national chauvinist prejudice and boasts about it. Burk makes what she can in defence of Taylor's relationship with Beaverbrook; even so, it is clear that her heart is not really in it. Towards the end of his life Taylor fell into decrepitude and ultimate senility, still unreconciled to the slights, disdain and refusals he had received at the hands of the establishment. Burk quotes him thus: 'I've had an empty frivolous life and not done much that I wanted to do, writing in the void without any real belief in anything…I don't like other people much.' (p.362)

Taylor's personal tragedy was that he very much wanted the baubles that were denied to him, but at the same time was unwilling to undertake the personality and professional makeover that would have brought him acceptance—in other words he declined to embrace his own choices. As a historian he leaves very little permanent legacy apart from one text, *The Struggle for Mastery in Europe*. This remains an unrivalled survey in depth of the diplomacy of Europe during the pre-First World War era, though even then without any linkage to its social and economic foundations.

Willie Thompson is on the editorial board of Socialist History

Personalities in labour history

Ross M. Martin, *The Lancashire Giant: David Shackleton Labour Leader and Civil Servant* (Liverpool University Press, Liverpool, 2000) ISBN 0 85323 944 4, xv+222pp., £16.99pbk.

This biography of David James Shackleton charts the career of a Lancashire weaver, of but scant education, but great ability, whom circumstances propelled into a leading position in both the TUC and the nascent Labour Party in parliament. Then in 1910, aged 47, he abruptly abandoned his lofty position in the Labour movement, where he was widely tipped to be the future leader of the party, to become a middle-rank civil servant in the Home Office as senior labour advisor. Then in 1916 he was appointed to be permanent secretary of the newly formed Ministry of Labour, unprecedented for a working-class man, such posts being the preserve of Oxbridge graduates. Even in wartime it caused ructions in the civil service, with William Beveridge protesting the loudest! This detailed biography bears out the author's contention that Shackleton was far more representative of the Edwardian labour movement than those of his contemporaries like Keir Hardie or Ben Tillett, who have attracted much greater literary attention. His broad outlook, unlike theirs, reflected more closely the mainstream opinion of the weightiest section of the labour movement of that period, the skilled craftsmen, and the semi-skilled in mining and manufacturing. It characterised the general run of British trade union officials and members—what John Saville described as the 'ideology of labourism'.[1]

The backdrop to his story gives a new insight into the complex, uneasy, often hostile relationships between trade unionists, both 'old' and 'new', socialists in the SDF and ILP and the Liberal Party. The establishment in 1900 of the Labour Representation Committee (LRC), still found many 'old guard' unions clinging to Liberal representation of their concerns in parliament, despite the feeble performance of such 'Lib-Lab' MPs. The Taff Vale judgement was to jerk such unions out of their complacency, opening the way for a party speaking for labour in parliament that was truly independent of the other two political parties. This was a principle that Shackleton consistently advocated publicly, and in union meetings, accepting the LRC parliamentary pledge of solidarity by signing its constitution, despite his inherent liberal sympathies. The harsh conditions of life in the cotton mills, where he started work aged nine as a 'half timer', was a background shared by many of his fellow trade union leaders, as was his nonconformity and abstemious habits, but he had other unique qualities that placed him head and shoulders above his contemporaries. Literally, being over 6 foot tall with a body in proportion, he was affectionately known as the 'gentle giant', later the 'Lancashire giant' when he became nationally known by the press. Shackleton's sheer physical presence, his striking appearance, lack of rhetoric or 'side' when speaking, made a tremendous impression on all who heard him. An imperturbable demeanour, great stamina giving him the capacity to seem tireless, were qualities that he needed as full-time secretary of the Darwen weavers' union involving patient negotiations on the complex piecerate system in the cotton trades. Good experiences for his future careers, starting with his unopposed win in the Clitheroe by election in 1902 at the age of 39. The LRC quickly endorsed Shackleton, who'd been nominated by the Textile Factory Workers' Association, who wanted 'one of our own' to represent them as an independent Labour MP, but without the tag 'socialist', which angered the socialists since Clitheroe was one of their strongholds in Lancashire. The Liberals after trying to divide the loyalties of the trade unionist, then failing to find a candidate of their own, withdrew. And as the Liberals were not contesting the seat, the Tories decided not to. Shackleton was a popular choice, with no less than eleven nomination papers all signed by fellow workers.

As one of the tiny group of four Labour MPs in the House of Commons he came in for close attention from the ILP and SDF looking for Liberal 'backsliding', and from the press keen to detect any socialist leanings. Shackleton was at great pains to explain that he was Labour, 'pure and simple' and 'as far as anything but Labour is concerned, my ideas are progressive'. These were far reaching: anti-picketing laws, workers' compensation, old-age pensions, the eight-hour day, electoral reform, free trade, women's suffrage, and reform of liquor licensing laws. All reforms he wanted to see, but he rejected the goals of socialism—not because they were unworthy; rather, too utopian and distant, diverting attention from more immediately achievable aims. On the other hand he did actively support socialist proposals for the nationalisation of land, railways canals, mines and minerals; all of which he regarded as being well within the sphere of practical politics. It is not without irony that what he regarded as 'a matter of pure business', is scorned as ideological 'baggage' today, by New Labour. The issue of women's suffrage gained much attention from the fact that the levy on cotton workers to pay Shackleton's election expenses and parliamentary salary would come largely from women workers, who were in the majority, but had no vote. Emmeline Pankhurst told him he should do something for women in return. This he did, giving great prominence to their claim to have a voice in government. In 1910 he introduced a private member's bill on the question that had a majority on its second reading but was defeated by the Liberal government at committee stage. He was a prominent member of the Women's Trade Union League, doing much to promote their cause, being particularly conscious of the Weavers Amalgamation (of which he was a president) as the only union to effectively organise women—45,000 of their 80,000 members—although they were grossly under-represented in the union leadership. In what might seem a contradiction, he saw the place of married women as in the home, but as a right, not an obligation. The key to making this possible, he insisted, was trade unionism that could win an adequate wage for their menfolk. And Shackleton saw trade unions as a moral force, urging regard for the condition of people outside their own ranks. As a leading member of the Rechabites temperance society, Shackleton also saw liquor as one of the greatest obstacles to progress in the trade union and labour movement, having no hesitation in expounding his views at every opportunity. On industrial relations he trod a delicate, though principled line, believing industrial peace to be a priority: 'strikes developed angry feelings', with workers suffering the most. At the same time he considered strikes as an essential trade union weapon. Careful preparation for them could gain an acceptable agreement in their shadow. An 'iron fist in a velvet glove'. Even after the 1906 'victory' of 30 Labour MPs and the passing of the Trades Disputes Act, Shackleton insisted it was trade unions that were the primary defence of the workers' interests, above that of Parliamentary Labour Party (PLP), strongly resisting any weakening of their role. New Labour please note! The role of the PLP was, in his eyes, strictly reformist, a view that he was very influential in promoting from his leading position on many of the Commons committees, as well as his authoritative voice in the House. Despite the final end of 'Lib-Labism' when the miners' group of MPs joined the PLP, he did not see Labour as a party of government for the foreseeable future. No doubt this prompted him to turn down the chairmanship of the PLP in 1907 for that of the TUC. His very pragmatism led him to try frequently to defuse the tensions between socialist ideals and reformers in the PLP by urging a 'Labour Alliance' to show a common front between the two factions, although there was never formally any such alliance. In many ways Shackleton acted as a 'bridge' to furthering understanding between the trade unions and a Labour Party at large with all its diverse elements, and the PLP.

What comes out clearly from this period was that all the MPs in the PLP were working class, and Labour really did represent labour. It is very impressive to read of Shackleton's involvement in so many causes; the Co-operative movement, Ruskin College, temperance groups, as well as championing extension of secular education, Irish home rule, and cheap rail fares for workers, to name but a few. As an MP he was always very accessible and accountable, never choosing to be sheltered by a private secretary, and would tour his constituency regularly. He had seemingly tireless energy, but for all his commitments, he would only rarely break his golden rule, to keep Sunday as a day of rest to spend at home with his wife and family. Martin advances a number of possible reasons for Shackleton's sudden decision to change course and become a civil servant; disillusionment at the turmoil in the trade unions in 1910, pressure of his parliamentary and other work, greater money and security, none of which really explain why satisfactorily. Nor has Shackleton himself given any clues, having left no memoir. But as a civil servant he continued to speak for organised labour as and when the occasion demanded it. His is a biography well worth reading, giving a fascinating new angle on the formative years of the British Labour Party.

Peter Kentfield is a member of the Socialist History Society

Note

1. John Saville in Robert Benewick et al. (eds), *Knowledge and Belief in Politics. The problem of ideology* (London, 1973), pp.215–216.

Economic policy meets ideology

Noel Thompson, *Left in the Wilderness: The Political Economy of British Democratic Socialism since 1979* (Acumen, London, 2002) ISBN 1 902683 54 4, 312pp., £14.95 pbk.

Readers of Thompson's *Political Economy and the Labour Party* (1996) will be familiar with the strengths of this, his most recent, analysis of British social democracy. The focus is where economic policy and ideology meet. The method is careful exegesis of the strengths and weaknesses of various schools of thought, programmes, and prescriptions promoted in and around the Labour Party. Though this means that Thompson often takes the 'First, Second, Third' approach, the textbook style gains in clarity where it loses in fizz. But don't look for originality here and don't be seduced by the author's 'end of history' conclusions.

Thompson's analysis takes us from the Alternative Economic Strategy (AES) to attempts to find a transnational alternative to resurgent neo-liberalism. In between, his assiduous research identifies and explicates a succession of left political economies, many of them responses to the perceived failures or shortcomings of their predecessors. These include municipal socialism, post-Fordist socialism, producer co-operatives, market socialism, supply-side socialism, and the stakeholder economy *a la* Hutton— but also Blair. While one might laugh at the comic wrong-headedness of some of these ideas, the record is also impressive testimony to the energy, determination and ingenuity of the search for a way out of domination by capital. One might also see the enduringly strong electoral support for left parties in Western Europe as evidence of a popular expression of the same thing. But Thompson announces at the outset that his 'trope is tragedy' because what he sees in the projects which he meticulously dismantles in this book is merely a 'desperate, frenetic and ultimately futile attempt' to save democratic socialism in an 'increasingly hostile material and ideological environment'.

No one would doubt that the political and economic conjuncture post-1979 was difficult for the left; but one is entitled to ask: why? In part the desperation and futility which Thompson perceives can be explained by the weaknesses of some of the ideas which the Labour left championed. His own treatment of 'municipal socialism', for example, is punctuated by expressions such as 'hobbit socialists' seeking 'to destroy the power of Mordor from the confines of the Shire'; 'an obfuscatory side-show'; all 'sound and fury signifying nothing'; 'an attempt to skin the tiger claw by claw'; and 'wishful thinking'. The higher hocus pocus of post-Fordist/flexible specialisation 'socialism' was similarly inept and perhaps even more demoralising because it fascinated some socialists on the margins of the Labour Party—erstwhile critics of capitalism—and turned them into champions of the 'new', and often merely destructive critics of the socialist tradition. Some of these 'newists' can still be found advising the Labour government.

But most of the desperation and futility which Thompson perceives in the democratic socialist project derives from the same source as the one which drove the newists. It depends upon the perception that 'globalisation' has fundamentally undermined democratic socialism. Thompson accepts this thesis and surprisingly—for someone who is both an historian and a political economist—talks of the 'obvious' ascendancy in 'performance' of the 'Anglo-American model'. This is an impressive deference before the 'facts' of the hour indeed. In my view the deductive logic of globalisation theory is just as flawed. An alternative reading might suggest that the problems encountered by social democracy since the early 1970s derive from a conjuncture of mass unemployment, low growth and high rates of inflation—just as they did in the 1920s and 1930s. Keynesianism broke down under these circumstances because it was only ever effective at the margin, in conditions of full or nearly full employment. Nevertheless, the welfare state economies of Western Europe have weathered the post-1973 storm fairly well. There is no evidence of their convergence to an 'Anglo-Saxon' gold standard. Their survival will depend on evidence that capitalist economic performance is enhanced by the European 'social model' and is competitive against the cheap labour model. Of course, democratic socialism as a complete transformation of capitalism can be ruled out for the foreseeable future. But many of the ideas surveyed by Thompson had more modest ambitions and there is nothing in the 'new' circumstances to rule out future progress of the sort they aimed for (in the taming of markets and the democratisation of civil society) in Western Europe, though it is admittedly difficult to imagine Britain in the vanguard of such changes.

John Callaghan is professor of politics at the University of Wolverhampton

SUBSCRIBE TO SOCIALIST HISTORY

Socialist History is published twice-yearly and features articles, book reviews, debates and correspondence on all aspects of socialist cultural and political history

Journal subscription rates for 2003

UK institutional subscription £30 pa
UK individual subscription £15 pa

Rest of World institutional subscription £40 pa
Rest of World individual subscription £20 pa

Send a cheque, payable to Rivers Oram Press, to Rivers Oram Press, 144 Hemingford Road, London N1 1DE.

Subscription enquiries to ro@riversoram.demon.co.uk

Join the Socialist History Society

Socialist History is the journal of the Socialist History Society. Members of the society receive two copies of the journal per year and all the society's occasional publications

Membership rates for 2003

UK individual membership £18 (£12 unwaged)
Overseas membership £22.50 (£17 unwaged)
Labour movement organisations £22

Send a cheque, payable to Socialist History Society, to the secretary, Socialist History Society, 50 Elmfield Road, Balham, London SW7 8AL. Membership enquiries to francisking@waitrose.com

Socialist History Society Conference

Dissent and the State

Institute of Historical Research
Senate House, Malet Street, London WC1
26–27 September 2003

Speakers include

Peter Hennessy on 'MI5 and the "Internal Threat" 1947–71'
Mark Seddon on 'Dissent makes a comeback'
Nina Fishman on Trade Unions

Plus **Hilary Wainwright, Christine Shawcroft, Brian Brivati, Trevor Carter, John Callaghan, Andrew Hemingway, Scott Lucas, Paul Auerbach** on themes including dissent and the Labour Party; anti-racist struggle; the suppression of culture; and illusions of the left

Conference fee £18 (£12 unwaged)

Details from **Willie Thompson**
School of Arts and Social Sciences
History Division
Northumbria University Lipman Building
Newcastle upon Tyne NE1 8ST
e-mail w.thompson@newpolitics.org.uk
tel. 0191 145 733